WORTH THE WAIT

Written by BRIAN MURPHY   Photography by BRAD MANGIN
With additional photography by Missy Mikulecky, Andy Kuno, Suzanna Mitchell, David Paul Morris and Brian Haux

The Giants stretched before the make-or-break final series of the regular season against the Padres.

Cody Ross greeted an ecstatic dugout after scoring the first run in Game 5 of the World Series on Edgar Renteria's epic home run.

The moment San Francisco Giants fans had dreamed of for 52 years: World Series Champions at last.

TABLE OF CONTENTS

An estimated one million fans packed downtown for the World Series victory parade and celebration at city hall.

FOREWORD BY BRIAN WILSON

Let's get down to brass tacks for a moment: 40 Spring Training games, 162 regular-season games in 180 days, and 15 playoff games. Add 45,000 fans per game and realize the entire franchise history came down to the final game of the regular season. For most, this would have been a stressful time. For us, this was just another day at the park.

This book captures that very essence of calmness. At the same time, you will see the diligence, agony, perseverance, focus, passion, blood, sweat, and tears that appear on every team member's face. Our success came down to belief. It was the ability to see the unseen. A way of focusing and knowing something to be true without physical evidence. It comes down to wanting to attain greatness and actually knowing you will. You may not know how or when, but you certainly believe that the end result will be success. San Francisco did not know how the season would specifically unfold, but we focused on becoming champions.

We will never be given too much to handle in our lifetimes. At first glance, situations may be overwhelming, but overall we are given the ability to manage them. If we want to be the best, we have to ask for it. We have to ardently strive for the insurmountable if we plan to reach the top. Some say it's arrogance; I say it's ignorance. It's the ignorance of negativity that allows us to move forward toward a positive outcome.

For baseball players, our worst fear is failure. But this game is based on failure. Who can fail the least is how this game operates. Unfortunately, when a negative emotion enters our mind, it festers and takes over a situation. Usually when you focus on what you don't want to happen, that very end result comes alive.

The absolute apex of the entire season was the parade down Market Street. The City came alive, and it was a moment where the Giants and our supporters could share the victory as one. Without the city of San Francisco and its support, the Giants are merely just another team in the grind. The energy inside the park and on King Street during the course of the season cannot be described briefly in words. It was more of an emotion at its highest volume.

Winning the World Series is every player's dream from the time they first pick up a baseball. All that an athlete can think of is reaching the top. Every thought and moment of a player's life is based on his performance reaching its pinnacle. You would think that having attained the highest form of reward in your profession, you would feel accomplished and more relaxed. Quite the opposite is true. Once you get the taste for blood, you want nothing more than to feed like the animal that you've become.

San Francisco Giants/Andy Kuno

Ultimately, there is no top. We are designed to progress toward the unfathomable. It is that very thinking that keeps discipline within our mental schematics. Although it is a never-ending quest, I dare you to tell an athlete otherwise. Peer closely . . . you may see a champion arise.

PREFACE BY BRIAN MURPHY & BRAD MANGIN

There was no way we were not doing this book. Days after the Giants delivered the elusive dream of a World Series championship, visions began to materialize of commemorating the greatest season in history of the team for which we both grew up rooting.

It made sense professionally: a photographer—with more than two decades of experience shooting myriad games, players, and moments on assignment for the likes of Major League Baseball and *Sports Illustrated*—collaborating with a writer by trade who has authored two books and now gets paid to talk about sports every weekday morning on KNBR, the Giants flagship station.

It also made sense personally. Not only do we share Giants season tickets at AT&T Park, but also we have a common frame of reference in boyhoods shaped by the faded, seam-ridden artificial-turf days at Candlestick Park in the late '70s, when being a Giants fan was less than cool. Gone were Mays, Cepeda, and Marichal. We showered an aging Willie McCovey with standing ovations, powered down Carnation chocolate malts on the coldest of nights, saw hot dog wrappers pinned by the wind against the cyclone outfield fence, and endured the pain of Dodger Ron Cey killing the Giants over and over again.

To think that, decades later, nicknames like the Freak, B-Weezy, Buster, Pat the Bat, and Huff Daddy would inexorably link two lifelong fans who grew up idolizing the Count, Jack the Ripper, Ho-Ho, Moon Man, Doody, and Mad Dog speaks to the ties that bind not just baseball fans, but also, specifically, Giants fans.

For us, no season had come close to topping the memories of 1978. Those Giants were our first love, the squad that rode a Little Orange Skateboard (pitcher Vida Blue's comparison of the Giants to Cincinnati's vaunted Big Red Machine) all through a season of contention, providing meaning to a summer for a couple of young and impressionable Giants fans.

We have our personal treasured mementos from that year: Brad still has the ticket stub from Jacket Day on May 28, 1978, when Mike Ivie's grand slam helped beat the Dodgers, and Brian still has the photos he took with a Kodak Instamatic, on Picture Day that same year, of Joe Altobelli, Heiti Cruz, and Johnnie LeMaster on the field.

The seeds of 1978 flowered in our hearts and minds. We were rewarded with flashes of brilliance—the Humm Babies, Dusty's Thugs, a miracle of a new ballpark—and we stood sentinel even through the searing pain. We knew the A's were better in 1989, and we're still not entirely over 2002.

Brian Murphy flying the orange and black at home with his mom in the late '70s, top; Brad Mangin poses with Jack Clark at Candlestick Park on Picture Day in 1982, bottom.

Then came 2010, inexplicable, out of nowhere, destroying our long-held notions of Giants agony and shortcoming. When we held our season ticket draft over beers and laughs in the Spring, there was simply no way—*no way!*—we thought we'd be divvying World Series tickets six months later. Such is the beauty of the game and of personalities and talents and fans coming together in the most unexpected and glorious of ways.

The Giants won the World Series, and there was no way we were not doing a book. We hope you're glad we did.

INTRODUCTION BY MIKE KRUKOW & DUANE KUIPER

I think about San Francisco winning its first World Series every day. Everybody in the Giants organization does too, as do countless fans. There are so many memories to relive from that magical season; thankfully they are all captured in the pages that follow.

How about that game in L.A. when Bruce Bochy caught Don Mattingly going to the mound twice in one visit? From that day on, people started to pay attention and give Bochy more credit than they might have in the past. He got this bunch together despite having to constantly juggle the lineup. I would not be surprised if the Giants had 127 different lineups last season. That's incredible. I bet the Phillies had maybe 5.

Then there's the Cody Ross story. He's got style. He's not a big guy, but he lets it fly. He plays defense, he's got a good arm, and to get hot right when he did? It's something you ask the baseball gods: Can I get hot—and stay hot—through October? They certainly seemed to oblige.

What about the Sunday finale of the four-game set in San Diego in mid-September? When Buster Posey hit that first-inning home run off Padres ace Mat Latos, it was game on. The Padres had the matchup they wanted, but before you could blink the Giants were leading 2–0. Giants fans deserve a lot of credit for that series, as they took over that ballpark, and I assure you that did not go unnoticed by either team.

I'm glad this book will preserve these memories and images for the fans because the fans were such a huge part of the Giants story in 2010. I can honestly say that I have never enjoyed a game more than Game 2 of the World Series. The fans were singing to Journey, the attitude and energy were all about embracing the team, and that was as big a party as I have ever seen. That is until the parade.

The parade and celebration at city hall brought together the largest group of happy people I have ever seen or imagined. They lit up Northern California that morning. I tried to explain to my sister on the phone what it was like to be on Montgomery Street: your head would've had to have been on a swivel to take in all the sights and sounds.

I really do think about the fact that the Giants won the World Series every day. I was killing time one day with my iPad, onto which I've downloaded all five World Series games. I love that I can go to the seventh inning of Game 5 within a matter of seconds. Yesterday I watched Renteria's home run again. Today in Starbucks I watched it twice more. I can't help but wonder: Am I going to do this 15 years from now? Am I ever going to get over this?

A random Giants fan in Starbucks saw me watching the highlight and asked, "Are you watching the World Series?" "I am," I said, "and I'm not going to apologize."

—DUANE KUIPER

In late August of 2010, shortly after the Giants had fallen six and a half games back in the National League West, I went on the radio and said the Giants would win the division. People reacted as if I was an idiot. But the Giants always knew they'd come together. Some teams panic when they lose a series; the Giants never did that.

In baseball, you have to feel that if you do what you need to do, the ship will get on course. The Giants truly felt this, and come September, when the arms were steamrolling, they were like a snowball coming down a mountain and picking up speed. There was so much drama going into the final game of the regular season against the Padres, but no one in the Giants clubhouse ever thought they weren't going win. That's because of all the great characters you'll see and read about in this book.

That confidence came from guys like Pat Burrell, who said: *We can do this*. Think about his ride from the first overall pick in the draft to a guy sitting home on the couch who suddenly gets a second chance from the team he rooted for as a kid. That's huge. Burrell had won a World Series, and when he got the Giants clubhouse listening to him, he was fantastic.

Confidence came from Edgar Renteria, who said: *We have the team.* Struggling badly in the middle of the season, he went to manager Bruce Bochy and admitted he was playing terribly, but Bochy told him, sincerely, "We need you." And he was right.

It came from guys like Juan Uribe, who said: *This is going to happen.* Uribe is a fighter, and that's contagious in a clubhouse. There were so many games when the Giants were down, and Uribe was the last guy who could do something about it— and he did.

Brian Wilson was a mental stud. Matt Cain pitched like a finished product at age 26. Freddy Sanchez brought energy every day. Andres Torres played with urgency. Aubrey Huff kept things light—despite having toiled for nine big-league seasons without ever having won anything. The veterans had a tremendous influence on the young guys like Buster Posey, who made the Giants a better offensive team from day one, and that was huge for the team psyche. What Tim Lincecum did—resurrecting his season, breaking out a new pitch in September, dealing with the immense pressure, getting his attitude back—was simply amazing. His comeback was the most impressive feat of his career, and he is only going to get better.

The wonderful pictures and words in this book bring the memories rushing back, and yet the stories may be just beginning. After the Giants won the NL pennant in Philadelphia, I happened to be on a hotel elevator with Buster Posey. "I hope you know this doesn't happen every year," I said with a smile. Posey looked at me and said, "Why not?"

—MIKE KRUKOW

1 EARLY DAYS

The San Francisco Giants have been playing springtime baseball in Arizona since they were the New York Giants, drawn to the desert in 1947 by the lure of unspoiled air, wide open spaces and maybe the way the sunrise over the McDowell Mountains creates just the right splash of majestic orange in the otherwise purple dawn sky. It is a picture pretty enough to stare at, and to dream.

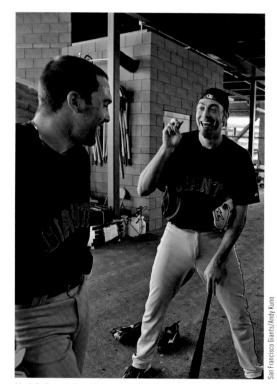

Mark DeRosa, left, with Jeremy Affeldt in Scottsdale, brought new energy to the Giants clubhouse.

In 2010, many things were familiar—the Scottsdale sunrise, the orange and black caps and jerseys, the rituals of morning drills, the Spring Training pilgrims—however, something was different. For the first time in half a decade, the Giants assembled for the Cactus League following a winning season. Eighty-eight victories in 2009 meant the Giants had reason to believe they could play winning ball. That they had done so, and planned to do so again, on the strength of a brilliant young pitching staff headlined by two-time Cy Young Award–winner Tim Lincecum ran counter to a franchise legacy fueled on the legendary bats of Mays, McCovey, and Cepeda; Clark, Williams, and Mitchell; Bonds and Kent.

Perhaps more important: the Giants brought to the ballpark new intangibles, positive things, a lightness of being. A new sound—laughter—was heard. New voices, too. Veterans Aubrey Huff and Mark DeRosa signed on to help Bengie Molina and Pablo Sandoval carry the offense, but Huff and DeRosa's arrival also meant the infusion of personality and charisma. The charge of energy was instant.

Asked if this seeming team-wide camaraderie meant anything of substance, Huff responded with an answer that would resonate all year: "I think so," he told writer Joan Ryan. "I've been on teams where you walk into a clubhouse, and it just doesn't feel right. I walked in here, and everyone's ragging on each other. Everybody seems to dish it out. And everybody takes it.

"Look at a guy like Lincecum. He doesn't have that 'I'm in the paper everyday' attitude," said Huff. "He hasn't let anything go to his head. So that sets a tone right there." Lincecum was more succinct as the team broke camp. "Everybody gets along," said the ace, just 25 years old on Opening Day.

For a team that had never won a World Series in its San Francisco history (the franchise's last title came in 1954, when the New York Giants were still relative newcomers to Spring Training in Arizona), goals seemed attainable, if heady. "We want to get into the playoffs," said Matt Cain, with five years service the longest-tenured Giant, about a team that hadn't been to the postseason since 2003. "And we want to go deep into October."

Not that a ballgame on April 5 could portend anything that might happen seven months later on the first night of November, but for those who believe in

The 2010 dream season began here, under the desert skies at Scottsdale Stadium.

The Kung-Fu Panda, Pablo Sandoval, was a consummate teammate and fan favorite.

mystical particles of energy, it is noteworthy that the Giants first win of 2010 came in the state of Texas, that the winning pitcher was Lincecum, that Brian Wilson nailed down the save, and that Edgar Renteria had a big day at the plate.

The Opening Day lineup that carried such hope contained names that would be absent come November: John Bowker—traded; Molina—traded; DeRosa—injured; Sandoval—benched. Still, the Giants swept the season-opening series from the Astros with wins by Lincecum, Barry Zito (No. 2 in manager Bruce Bochy's rotation), and Cain, giving the team its first 3–0 start since 2003 . . . and harbingers of things to come were anyone so inclined to look.

Opening Day in San Francisco marked the 11th season at the waterfront miracle that is AT&T Park. When Jerry Rice threw the ceremonial first pitch to Steve Young, fans wildly cheered the two symbols of San Francisco's last pro sports championship team, the 1994 49ers. That Friday afternoon game was a thriller: a 5–4, 13-inning win over the Atlanta Braves, with another jolt to remember from Renteria, who came out smoldering, going 11-for-16 in the first four games of the season. His two-run home run in the ninth inning off Braves closer Billy Wagner tied the game, lit up the crowd, and caused the veteran fireballer to opine after the game, "He's not hitting .700 for no reason."

But the baseball gods are nothing if not exacting. Following a hot 5–1 start to the season, things cooled

down on a road trip through Los Angeles and San Diego, in ways sickening (Aaron Rowand's beaning by the Dodgers' Vicente Padilla), depressing (fifth starter Todd Wellemeyer's loss to L.A. left him 0–2, with a 9.58 ERA), and hope-crushing (Manny Ramirez's two-run, game-winning home run on April 18).

Getting swept by the Padres in San Diego to cap a 1–5 trip—and scoring just four runs in three games—allowed grumblers to wonder if the Giants frustrated bats would ever be worthy of the team's stellar arms. A homestand in late April, during which the Giants took two of three from the two-time defending National League champion Philadelphia Phillies, provided a jolt of life, and the Giants finished the month with a record of 13–9; just one and a half games behind surprising San Diego.

John Bowker earned the Opening Day start in right field.

The momentum rolled on into May when Zito, historically slow to get going, beat the Florida Marlins on May 5 to improve to 5–0, his best start ever. With a 1.49 ERA that spoke to an effective slider, snappier fastball, and newfound confidence, Zito delivered, and Giants fans once again rocked AT&T Park with the familiar, if altogether different, chant of *BAR-RY! BAR-RY!*

But then, more Padres. Exactly what it was about those blue-and-gray-clad interlopers from the Gaslamp Quarter may never be defined, but the Padres proved more than ready for the Giants in 2010. San Diego's underrated pitching stymied the Giants again in a three-game sweep in mid-May, this time in San Francisco. The Padres' big young right-hander,

Mat Latos, sporting a sinister sneer beneath his low-pulled hat, finished things off in dominating fashion with a one-hitter.

On the TV pregame show the next day, Giants broadcaster Duane Kuiper, citing a litany of early-season one-run games and low-scoring nail-biters, first said, "Giants baseball... torture!" Teeth gnashed across the Bay Area, and fans called for the Giants to bring up hot-hitting catcher Buster Posey from the minors. A bounce-back three-game home sweep of the Astros quelled some of the frustration, the highlight coming when Wilson nailed down a Saturday save after a 15-pitch duel with Houston second baseman Kaz Matsui.

The torture was only beginning. The Giants won just once on a seven-game road trip to San Diego, Arizona, and Oakland. It was a final line of demarcation, with the low point of May coming with a three-game sweep inflicted by the A's in Oakland. The much-criticized Giants offense scored exactly one run in 27 innings. A's fans crowed, piling on their penchant for taunting Giants fans with scoreboard reminders that no World Series titles had ever come to San Francisco.

Giants fans seethed. The clubhouse fell stone silent. On May 6, San Francisco sat alone in first place in the division and seven games over .500; now, 17 days later, the Giants had slipped to a record of 22–21 and three games back in the standings. Something had to be done.

Previous pages, left to right: **Todd Wellemeyer, Eugenio Velez, Eli Whiteside, and DeRosa all made early season contributions;** above, **a young fan in search of a coveted autograph.**

Barry Zito's sizzling 5–0 record and 1.49 ERA helped the Giants get off to a quick start.

McCovey Cove on April 26, 2010, the night the Giants beat Roy Halladay and the Phillies 5–1.

Aaron Rowand enjoyed a productive April before a beaning landed him on the disabled list.

Sandoval and Andres Torres celebrated a sweep of the Houston Astros, left; Freddy Sanchez made an immediate impact when he returned to the lineup in May, right.

Sandoval's expression embodied the frustration of a Giants team that scored one run in three straight losses at Oakland in May.

On a glorious November afternoon in downtown San Francisco, Aubrey Huff—in the middle of the World Series celebration at city hall and in front of the mayor, team owners, and nearly one million cheering Giants fans—pulled red thong underwear from his pants, held it aloft, and shouted, "This thing nailed it! The Rally Thong is going to the Hall of Fame!"

In that moment, it was hard to imagine that this power-hitting savior, the heart of the clubhouse and life of the party, was the same guy whose signing 10 months earlier had been viewed as a last resort. It was no secret that the Giants had sought numerous options for first base, but Huff, longing to erase his name from third place on the list of active players who had logged the most career games without reaching the playoffs (1,479), saw promise enough to accept a one-year offer to join the Giants.

Questions lingered about Huff's hitting just 15 home runs in 2009 after blasting 32 the year before. When asked about AT&T Park's hitter-unfriendly reputation, the quick-witted Huff said, "If Barry Bonds can hit home runs there, I can, too, right?" Huff's first home run in China Basin was an inside-the-park job, and he did not stop until he led the team with 26 home runs, 86 RBI, and a .385 on-base percentage. He proved his worth in key moments—a game-tying single in the ninth inning of the NLDS Game 3 in Atlanta; scoring the winning run on a sacrifice fly in Game 4 of the NLCS; belting a key home run in the World Series Game 4 win in Texas—but Huff's value ran deeper.

He was versatile, playing three different defensive positions without a gripe. Moreover, he was a clubhouse fulcrum. He kept it light. He jokingly welcomed phenom Buster Posey as "Jesus," with the Spanish pronunciation. He called rookie Madison Bumgarner "a country redneck—and I mean that as a compliment." Huff urged the Giants to sign his college teammate and friend, Pat Burrell, then dubbed their mutual defensive presence as the "Water Buffalo" outfield.

Huff's greatest contribution—or at least his most indelible—came with 30 games left to play and pennant pressure mounting when he first donned the red Rally Thong and predicted the team would finish with a record of 20–10. When he doubled in a key run in the final game of the season to clinch the division title, they'd done just that. The Giants—and Huff, at last—had reached the playoffs.

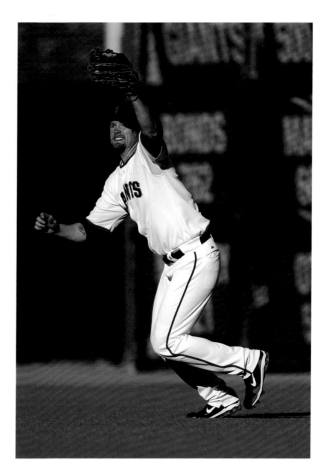

On Friday night, May 28, 2010, Gerald Dempsey Posey sat in a Utah hotel room. Earlier in the day, "Buster," a family nickname, had led the Giants Triple-A Fresno Grizzlies to an 8–0 shellacking of the Salt Lake Bees, raising his batting average to .349 in the process. When the telephone rang and Posey heard the voice of Grizzlies manager Steve Decker, the news that had become all but inevitable could not have come as a shock: Buster Posey had been called up to the big league club.

The Giants needed the help. Two days earlier San Francisco had suffered a demoralizing loss to the Washington Nationals. Lincecum walked five batters and did not make it out of the fifth inning, though the ace was not alone in contributing to a skid that dropped the Giants to fourth place in the NL West. Things felt dire, even before Memorial Day.

Sporting a close-cropped crew cut that emphasized his apple-cheeked youth, Posey arrived at AT&T Park for a Saturday night game against the Arizona Diamondbacks and donned the cream-colored No. 28 jersey. He shined in front of 37,400 fans ready to embrace him, roping three singles and driving in three runs in a 12–1 win. In his first at bat, Posey lined a two-out, RBI single to center field to score Freddy Sanchez: precisely the kind of disciplined situational hitting the Giants had been missing. Following his third hit of the night, as Posey stood at first base with cheers washing over him, coach Roberto Kelly leaned in and said, "It's that easy, huh?" "No," Posey answered, "it isn't."

Giants fans hadn't felt this kind of pride in a homegrown position player in what seemed like forever. The heroes of the recent past—Barry Bonds, Jeff Kent, J.T. Snow, Rich Aurilia—were all acquired either via trade or free agency. It was the first time in nearly 25 years—since 1986 when former No. 1 pick Will Clark made his debut and the following season when farmhand Matt Williams came up—that Giants fans experienced this unique, warm rush of excitement.

Posey's immediate impact threw a lifeline to manager Bruce Bochy, who had been swamped with issues

Called up in late May, Buster Posey fulfilled the promise that inspired the Giants to make him a first round draft pick.

regarding his lineup card. Mark DeRosa had been expected to be an RBI man in the five-hole in the batting order, but he was lost for the season to wrist

Traded to the Texas Rangers in July, Bengie Molina would face his former team come October.

2009 trade deadline had Giants fans justifiably concerned about general manager Brian Sabean's move. But Sanchez's productive return made him look like a savior and Sabean a sage. Four days after penciling Sanchez back in the lineup, Bochy inserted Andres Torres into the leadoff spot in a game against Oakland. The kinetic center fielder provided an instant spark that contributed to the Giants winning 14 of their next 20 games.

The overhaul continued with Sabean's late-May surprise signing of Pat Burrell. A Bay Area kid from Boulder Creek in Santa Cruz County, Burrell starred at Bellarmine Prep high school in San Jose and the University of Miami before being drafted No. 1 overall in 1998 by the Phillies, with whom he earned a World Series ring in 2008. Pat the Bat moved to Tampa Bay in 2009, but his production fell, and in May 2010 the Rays gave Burrell his outright release. Fans longing for more hitting wondered why the Giants would want a guy whose .202 batting average suggested a player in decline. The Giants viewed signing Burrell to a minor league contract as a no-risk deal, and after a week of watching him exhibit impressive bat speed in Triple-A, they called him up.

Bochy started Burrell in Pittsburgh on June 5. Despite the sting of having been released by Tampa Bay, Burrell said he "couldn't be happier" to be playing for his favorite boyhood team. The following week, on a Friday night versus Oakland at AT&T Park, Burrell ignited an orange-clad crowd with a go-ahead, two-run home run—his first as a Giant—powering the Giants to a satisfying sweep over the A's. When closer Brian Wilson escaped a bases-loaded eighth inning and delivered a five-out piece of work to save Sunday's final game, the Giants had returned the favor from May's embarrassing sweep in Oakland, and Giants fans had the last laugh on their East Bay rivals.

surgery in May. Injuries also hobbled Edgar Renteria, who took all of 10 at bats between May 6 and June 19. Following a sensational rookie season, Pablo Sandoval struggled at the plate, going five weeks from April into May without hitting a home run.

The skipper was known for his even-keel professionalism and stoic detachment from the game's daily dramas, but Bochy was stuck. Then Posey arrived, which helped immeasurably, as did other fortuitously timed developments. On May 19, Freddy Sanchez finally made his 2010 debut. The Giants expected their second baseman to play slick defense and handle the bat in the two-spot; however, Sanchez's persistent injuries since being acquired from Pittsburgh at the

Bochy now had his center fielder and leadoff man. He had his No. 2 hitter and stalwart second baseman. He had the ready-for-prime-time rookie and a legitimate power threat. As expected, pitching provided the ballast through May and June. While Lincecum worked through an uncharacteristic rough patch, during which he walked 15 batters in three starts in May and lost a marquee duel with Colorado's Ubaldo Jimenez on Memorial Day, Matt Cain delivered. Over five starts in late May and early June, Cain went 4–1 with a 0.44 ERA, allowing just two runs in a 41-inning stretch. Riding a deceptive release point and repeatable motion, Cain said he was simplifying things, growing into a better pitcher. Bochy, who saw his share of greats in nine seasons as a big league catcher, marveled at what he called Cain's "maniacal focus."

Storm clouds gathered once more when the Red Sox came to town in late June. Packed houses saw the Giants take the Friday opener, and then Boston evened the series with a win on Saturday. On a warm and sunny Sunday, the highly anticipated showdown between Lincecum and Red Sox ace Jon Lester went to the visitors, as Boston cuffed around Lincecum, who gave up three walks, five hits, a home run, and four earned runs in just three innings of work. Losing two of three to Boston was tough, but what happened next cut deep: a sweep at home at the hands of the rival Dodgers. The starters and relievers came up short, the hitters scored just six runs in three games, and the Dodgers passed the Giants in the NL West standings.

June ended with San Francisco posting a 13–14 losing record. The Giants would begin July in Denver, the first stop on a three-city swing leading into the All-Star break. An 11-game, broiling summer road trip appeared daunting for a team losing its stride, but as the Giants plane took off for Colorado, major changes were already in the air.

Portending a bright future, Posey caught fellow rookie Madison Bumgarner for the first time in the big leagues on June 26.

Pablo Sandoval became a fixture at the hot corner, ranking second on the Giants in both games played and also innings played.

The Giants surpassed the three million mark in attendance for the ninth time in 11 seasons in China Basin.

Jonathan Sanchez allowed the fewest hits per nine innings in the National League, left; Jeremy Affeldt and the Giants bullpen posted a 2.99 ERA in 2010, right.

Posey made the challenging transition to every day catcher and cleanup hitter look easy.

The youngest pitcher ever to start a game in his Major League debut for the San Francisco Giants, Bumgarner averaged seven strikeouts per nine innings in 18 starts.

Manager Bruce Bochy navigated a season filled with unpredictable challenges.

Staff ace Tim Lincecum worked through mid-season struggles and delivered another All-Star performance, leading the Giants in wins and strikeouts.

Bay Area native Pat Burrell joined the Giants in May, left; reunited with good friend and college teammate Aubrey Huff, Pat the Bat thrived, right.

He spent 12 character-testing years in the minors. He started the 2009 season in the rookie league—at age 31. He made the Giants 2010 Opening Day roster, though only just, as a reserve outfielder. On paper, Andres Torres was an unlikely candidate to earn the team's highest honor. But on October 1, before a Friday night sellout crowd tingling with the possibility of the Giants clinching the NL West, Torres graciously accepted the Willie Mac Award, voted on by the players and presented annually to their most inspirational teammate. The moment validated the journey, richly and sweetly. "He inspired the team," said Willie McCovey that night. "It's hard not to like him."

A gritty player who bounced through five organizations, Torres perhaps best defined the 2010 Giants. Few figured the Giants to end the year as World Series champions; fewer still foresaw Torres being the engine at the top of the lineup. Given his chance because of Mark DeRosa's season-ending injury and Aaron Rowand's slump, Torres answered Bruce Bochy's call with resounding fervor. To say he hit .263 with a .343 on-base percentage, ranked fourth in the league in doubles and tenth in extra-base hits, and delivered an unexpected 16 home runs is to define Torres numerically; however, he is better defined aesthetically. Torres's defense was sensational, and the speed that had made him a teenage track star in

Puerto Rico served him well not only in the spacious outfield of AT&T Park, but also on the base paths. He was a sight: arms pumping, hands chopping the air, his thick gold necklace bouncing off his jersey as he motored from first base to third or swiped second with one of his team-high 26 steals.

In the clubhouse, teammates marveled at a player whose team-first attitude, hard work, and sincerity wasn't just restricted to his earnest interviews with reporters. His open personality included crediting his recent career surge to treatment for attention deficit disorder, diagnosed in 2007. His naturally friendly demeanor led Aubrey Huff to guess that Torres says hello at least seven or eight times a day. Torres's toughness never came into question; an emergency appendectomy on September 12 left him feeling frustrated and helpless during the stretch run, but Torres battled back into the lineup and made a start in Colorado just two weeks later—and homered.

During a season that required unsung players to step up, Torres was undeniably clutch. He twice won games with walk-off hits, including an early-season tenth-inning line drive to right field that completed a four-hit game for Torres and a sweep of Arizona. Mobbed by his teammates, Torres proclaimed it his "best day in the big leagues." Granted, that was before he delivered a late-October RBI double in the seventh inning of Game 4 of the World Series and won it all the next night.

THE CHANGES

The summer of 2010 conjures so many images and memories, with so many ballplayers etching their names and exploits into eternal memory. Think Madison Bumgarner, 20 years young, called up from Triple-A in late June and ripping off four straight wins with his strong, elastic left arm. Think Travis Ishikawa, handed his first start in more than six weeks on July 3 in Colorado and answering with a thunderous grand slam off Rockies ace Ubaldo Jimenez—as unexpected as it was marvelous—to end a seven-game losing streak. And yet the most startling performance of all was turned in by a man whose name never once appeared in a box score.

Thanks to savvy scouting that landed first round draft picks
Madison Bumgarner, above, and **Tim Lincecum,** right, **the Giants possess the best young pitching staff in baseball.**

General manager Brian Sabean was an easy target for frustrated fans; true, the Giants had not made the playoffs since 2003, but the young team built on pitching had shown marked progress, improving their season win total by 16 games in 2009. In a show of confidence, managing general partner Bill Neukom gave Sabean, as well as manager Bruce Bochy, a two-year extension. Sabean responded by orchestrating a series of moves through July and August that would not only deliver San Francisco's first World Series championship, but also leave his vociferous critics bereft of ammunition.

The opening salvo came when Sabean traded Bengie Molina on July 1. While flying to Colorado following the humiliating end-of-June home sweep to the Dodgers, Sabean consummated a deal with the Rangers, sending Molina to Texas in return for reliever Chris Ray and a minor-league prospect. There was no denying that Molina was slumping, but it was a bold and risky move to cut him loose, as his spirit and leadership twice earned Molina the Giants prestigious Willie Mac Award. Molina was a well-liked veteran and a calming presence for the pitching staff, particularly for Lincecum, who was on record as saying he wished he could cut his Cy Young Awards in two and give half to Molina for his stewardship.

Sabean did not mince words. "Quite frankly, we've got to figure a way to get Buster in there on a more regular basis," he said, "and this allows us to do that."

It is exceedingly rare to see a rookie given the weighty responsibilities of both full-time catcher and cleanup hitter, but Posey responded with a roar. He launched a 21-game hit streak that fell one game shy of Willie McCovey's Giants rookie record, which helped the Giants kick down the doors in July. The team went 20–8, posting their highest monthly win total

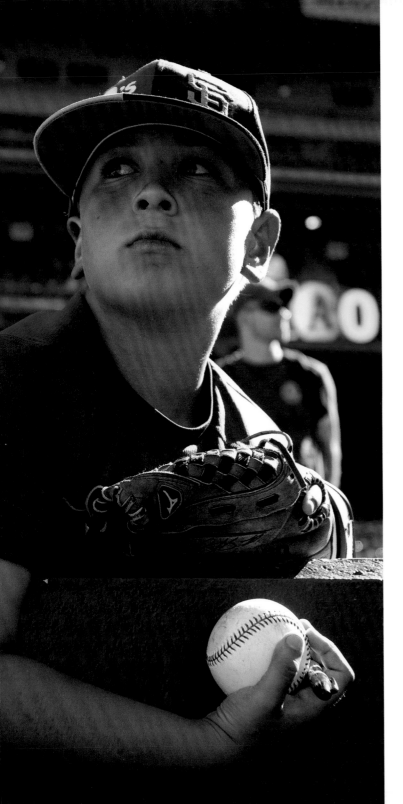

since September 2000. The outburst redefined their season, though not before the team endured some soul-searching moments.

The darkest day came after a 15-inning, five-hour-24-minute loss in Colorado on July 4. The Giants tied the game with three runs in the eighth inning and had their chances to win it in extra frames before losing on a sacrifice fly. The Giants dropped seven and a half games back in the standings; it would be their deepest deficit of the 2010 season, but inside the Giants clubhouse, a pulse still beat. Pat Burrell, a veteran of playoff runs, reassured Aubrey Huff, his old college pal who had never reached the postseason in 10 big-league seasons, "If we just pick up one game a week on the Padres, we'll be fine."

Seasons can plummet amid such strife. Or sometimes, inexplicably, seasons can soar. So it was that the Giants grew wings on July 5 in Milwaukee, when starter Jonathan Sanchez pitched six innings of one-run ball for his seventh win of the season. San Francisco swept the Brewers four straight, Posey hit his first Major-League grand slam, Bumgarner notched his first win in the bigs, and the Giants barreled into the All-Star break winning six of seven, putting them four games back of San Diego.

San Francisco sent closer Brian Wilson and Tim Lincecum to the All-Star Game in Anaheim. Lincecum became the first Giant since Juan Marichal to make three straight Midsummer Classics, while Wilson bubbled with adrenaline over his second selection. Despite the American League's having won 12 straight (not including the controversial tie game in 2002), Wilson was optimistic, saying, "That would be epic if we had home-field advantage for the World Series—as Giants."

In an emotional series at Dodger Stadium shortly after the All-Star break, Bochy rocked the rivalry when he called out Dodgers acting manager Don Mattingly for violating rule 8.06. The Giants skipper noted to the umpires that Mattingly's ninth-inning visit to closer Jonathan Broxton actually constituted *two* visits; after speaking to Broxton on the mound, Mattingly stepped away, then briefly doubled back and returned to give his pitcher a final piece of advice, thereby making his second trip to the mound in the inning, which by rule requires the pitcher's removal from the game. It was brilliant, audacious, and just the sort of competitive adrenaline that the Giants needed. The Dodgers players and fans watched in stunned dismay as Broxton left the field with Giants runners at second and third and San Francisco down one run. The rejuvenated Giants rallied for a 7–5 win.

It was one of the most exhilarating games of the season, but the Giants weren't done picking on their longtime foes. A week later, the Dodgers traveled north. They had owned China Basin in recent years, but Lincecum won the first game; Burrell won the second with a two-run home run off Broxton; and when Wilson closed a gem started by Cain, the Giants fans cheered with unadulterated happiness: for the first time since 2003, the orange and black swept the blue in San Francisco.

On the same day as Burrell's blast, Sabean delivered the bullpen much-needed relief with deadline deals for left-handed specialist Javier Lopez from Pittsburgh and right-handed setup man Ramon Ramirez from Boston. Sabean wasn't done. In mid-August he bolstered the middle infield by trading for Mike Fontenot from the Cubs then added a power bat by acquiring veteran slugger Jose Guillen from the Royals. On August 22 Sabean put in a waiver claim for Florida outfielder Cody Ross—for the express purpose of blocking the Padres from claiming him. When the Marlins unexpectedly awarded Ross to the Giants, Sabean had acquired his seventh new player of the season and a sixth outfielder on a team that already had plenty.

After a less-than-stellar trip to Atlanta, the normally quiet Jonathan Sanchez made the brazen proclamation that the Giants were playoff bound. It seemed a stretch, as the team played in fits and starts.

Pat Burrell hit two home runs in an August win over the Cubs, including this, a grand slam.

Another series loss to the Padres was particularly frustrating. The Giants did manage to erase a nine-run deficit in a sprawling late-August game against the Cincinnati Reds—only to lose 12–11 in extra innings. In the next game, Lincecum lost to Arizona and finished a cold-sweat nightmare of a month: zero wins against five losses and a 7.82 ERA. Then on August 30, Ross froze when Colorado's Carlos Gonzalez hit a broken-bat flare in the ninth inning

of a tight game the Giants led 1–0. The unlikely hit soared over Ross's head and led to a crushing 2–1 loss to the Rockies. Fans who did not yet know Ross or his capabilities grumbled in pain, though none took the loss harder than Ross. "Broken-bat triple," he said in a quiet clubhouse. "Never seen anything like it."

After having entered August just a game and a half back of the Padres, the turbulent month saw the Giants now five games back. But on the final night of

the month, Bumgarner delivered a mighty six innings of one-run ball. His rookie battery mate Posey doubled and drove in two; Freddy Sanchez had a pair of hits; Torres homered; Wilson earned the save; and instead of recoiling in anguish after the "broken-bat triple" loss, the Giants rebounded and beat the Rockies. Meanwhile, the Padres were stumbling; that very night, San Diego, who had endured but one three-game losing streak all season, lost its sixth straight game.

Brian Wilson, showing early signs of his infamous beard, and Tim Lincecum represented the Giants at the 2010 All-Star Game in Anaheim.

Bruce Bochy congratulated Wilson after pitching a scoreless inning; the National League's victory would clinch home field advantage in the World Series for the Giants.

Lefthander Jonathan Sanchez enjoyed a banner year in 2010, winning a career-high 13 games.

Buster Posey hit a double to lead off the 11th inning then scored the winning run in a key victory over the first-place Padres in August.

Guillermo Mota earned the win on the last day of July, pulling the Giants within a game and a half of the division lead.

Every member of the 2010 Giants contributed to the team's success; clockwise from top left: reliever Chris Ray, who came from Texas in the Bengie Molina deal; Bay Area-born Nate Schierholtz; trade deadline acquisition Ramon Ramirez; and defensive specialist Travis Ishikawa.

Posey proved a natural in assuming the role of every day catcher, *left*; Andres Torres flourished as leadoff hitter and regular center fielder, *right*.

Sergio Romo led the Giants in allowing the fewest walks and hits per innings pitched, left; Juan Uribe came through in the clutch time and again, right.

Not to overstate the appeal of Buster Posey's work-first, talk-later, clean-cut, team-oriented, fundamentally sound appeal, but when the local boy made good enough to serve as grand marshal of the 2010 Leesburg Spirit of Christmas Parade in his small Georgia hometown (pop. 2,965), a reporter for the local newspaper wrote: "It seemed that many more children were interested in seeing the Giants catcher than the jolly old man from the North Pole." Yes, Virginia, there is a Buster.

In the 2008 MLB draft, the Giants brass leaped to make Posey the fifth overall selection. Snagging the Florida State star and winner of the Golden Spikes Award as the nation's best collegiate player would prove a key moment in franchise history. Despite playing the first two months of the 2010 season in the minors, Posey fended off a magnificent NL rookie class, edging Atlanta's Jason Heyward to become Rookie of the Year, San Francisco's first since John Montefusco in 1975.

Voters rewarded Posey as much for hitting as for his deft shepherding of baseball's best pitching staff to the mountaintop. His pure hitting stroke delivered a .305 batting average, 18 home runs, and 67 RBI in just 108 games. More impressive still: baseball stat gurus place great weight on OPS, or on-base plus slugging, which represents the sum of on-base percentage and slugging percentage. Posey did not make his big-league debut until May 29 yet still ranked fifth behind the likes of three-time league MVP Albert Pujols and 2010 MVP Joey Votto.

His teammates marveled at Posey's leadership gene. When he arrived in San Francisco, he coolly handled the media hordes with drama-free statements, leaving the impression of a player more seasoned than his resume showed. One scout went so far as to liken watching Posey walk onto the baseball diamond to watching Larry Bird walk onto the basketball court. "I just expect myself to work hard every day," said the rookie, "and when the game comes around, I try and help this team get wins."

That statement might as well have been engraved over Posey's locker. During a torrid July, Posey's 21-game hit streak, team-record 43 hits for the month and sizzling .441 batting average led the Giants to 20 wins in 28 games and earned Posey NL Player of the Month honors in the process. "I've been concentrating on winning ballgames," Posey told reporters with characteristic humility after his hit streak ended on July 29. "It's nice the attention can go back to that."

Posey's exploits are all over the Giants 2010 highlight reel: a clutch home run off Padres ace Mat Latos on the road to nail down a key series win in September, another jack against San Diego in his final regular-season at bat to vanquish the Padres en route to the Giants winning the NL West, the four-hit game in Game 4 of the NLCS against the favored Phillies, the World Series Game 4 blast in Texas. Fans swooned for the

natural who summoned images of heroes past. In just four short months, Posey, the first rookie catcher to win a World Series in more than 40 years, established himself as one of the most popular players to don the orange and black.

"He's gonna be a superstar in this league," Aubrey Huff proclaimed. "Just you watch."

Can the simple act of turning a calendar page change the fate of one man—or 25 for that matter? Or can destiny be forged with pure will, guts, and skill? Whether by indefinable magic or the meshing of the most talented pitching staff in baseball and an unexpected collection of unselfish achievers, the 2010 Giants made September 1 their launch pad to greatness.

Tim Lincecum took the mound that night, his future uncertain—if the harshest of doubters were to be believed. Everything about Lincecum came into question: his velocity, his health, his future, even the length of his hair. Great competitors answer calls at times like this, and Lincecum's line that night—eight innings, nine strikeouts and but one run allowed—stirred something in the fans, who sensed a larger force at work. Ovations at the close of innings grew louder. Timmy the Kid was back.

Adding to the aura was the Giants having won that game on the heroics of—Darren Ford? Bruce Bochy summoned Ford, called up from Double-A that day, to pinch-run in the eighth inning of a 1–1 game. Lincecum sacrificed Ford to second, and when Ford broke for third, Rockies catcher Miguel Olivo airmailed the throw into left field. Thunder erupted in the stands as Ford sprinted home with the winning run. "It felt like the World Series," said Ford.

That same night the Padres lost their seventh straight game.

The ensuing month proved legendary for the Giants. The team's 18–8 record in September could not begin to measure the wellspring of emotion that gripped the Bay Area, especially over the stretch of 18 consecutive games during which Giants pitchers never allowed more then three runs, a mark not matched in baseball since 1917.

Singling out the best Giants win down the stretch is like trying to choose the best view in The City. A strong candidate: Saturday, September 4, in Los Angeles. After dropping the Friday opener, San Francisco trailed the next night 4–0. Inspiration struck in the seventh inning when Buster Posey homered deep into the bleachers off Ted Lilly. Edgar Renteria took Lilly deep in the eighth. Dodgers reliever Octavio Dotel fared no better, surrendering a blast to pinch hitter Pat Burrell. Still leading 4–3 heading into the ninth, L.A. notched one out before Cody Ross hustled out an infield single. When Juan Uribe deposited a Dotel pitch deep into the night, the Giants took the lead for good, and the dugout erupted. "It's funny

Fans had plenty of reasons to cheer as the Giants kicked things into high gear in September.

to see guys in the league 10 years, guys 35 years old, acting like little kids," said Posey of the dugout/mosh pit. Aubrey Huff added, "Seems like every homer [Uribe] hits has been late—and big." Broadcaster Mike Krukow would call September 4 the "igniter."

After toiling 10 years in the big leagues without experiencing the playoffs, Aubrey Huff kept the Giants focused reaching the postseason.

After describing himself on Jim Rome's ESPN TV talk show as a mental assassin and certified ninja, closer Brian Wilson acted the part that Saturday night, nailing down the game, then flaunting both his 39th save and an ever-growing, ever-darkening beard. Meanwhile, the Padres lost their ninth game in a row. The next night, Jonathan Sanchez beat the Dodgers with seven shutout innings, and when the Padres' losing skid reached double digits, the Giants were a single game back, having made up five and a half games in less than two weeks.

After winning a three-game series in Arizona, San Francisco arrived in San Diego ready to exorcise the Padres demons that had haunted the Giants all season. Many believed the four-game set would portend the outcome of their respective seasons. The convergence of this Giants team's charisma plus September momentum resulted in a stunning invasion of Petco Park, as thousands of emboldened Giants fans, drawn like believers on a pilgrimage, made the trek south and filled San Diego's ballpark with interloper energy.

The Giants responded in kind. In the opener, Uribe, Posey, Huff, and Burrell all lashed home runs— and not dinks that just cleared the fence, but rather savage, angry bombs. Huff won game two with his legs; after being hit by a pitch, Huff stole second, made a daring take of third on a fielder's choice to shortstop, and then scored the game's only run on a ground ball to third. After Saturday's one-run squeaker loss, the Sunday finale saw Posey start things off with a first-

inning two-run message home run off nemesis Mat Latos, while Lincecum stymied the Padres with nine strikeouts and one run in seven innings to earn the win. Of the six series in which the two teams squared off, it would be the only one all year that the Giants would take from the Padres.

Tied for first place and knowing that the season ended with three games against San Diego at AT&T Park made the next couple of weeks rife with anxiety, but the Giants did not let up. Sanchez beat L.A. again, blowing away the Dodgers with 12 strikeouts. To the dulcet tones of Tony Bennett crooning post-victory, the faithful cheered the raising of the Giants banner to the top of the flagpole that presents the NL West teams in order of the standings. Bumgarner, looking less

Giants fans began to feel a sense of destiny as October approached.

and less like a rookie, threw seven shutout innings in a win at Wrigley Field. Uribe had six RBI against the Cubs—in one inning. The Giants buried the Rockies in Denver behind wins from Lincecum and Cain, who won the series finale at Coors Field on September 26 after taking a no-hitter into the eighth inning.

A sweep of the Diamondbacks put the Giants up three games with three to play against San Diego. Needing just one victory to clinch the division, the Giants made torture into the highest of art forms. Despite an emotional pregame appearance by an ailing Willie McCovey to present Andres Torres the Willie Mac Award before the first game, the Padres won 6–4. And despite a chance to clinch on national television on Saturday, the Padres won again, 4–2.

Sunday, October 3, dawned with an array of scenarios: the Giants could win the division . . . or the Wild Card . . . or tie the Padres and travel to San Diego for a playoff. That it was Latos, the merciless villain, for the Padres seemed right. That it was Sanchez, the brazen guarantor, for the Giants seemed equally right. The 42,822 fans who rocked the house along with the multitudes that watched on TV and listened on the radio will not soon forget pitcher Jonathan Sanchez getting the party started with a stunning triple in the third inning ("Let's watch Sanchez *GO!*" cried Duane Kuiper in the booth) and the lockdown pitching— *the pitching!*—by Santiago Casilla, Ramon Ramirez, Javier Lopez, Sergio Romo, and Brian Wilson.

When the closer struck out Will Venable to end it, then turned, crossed his arms, and looked to the sky—six whirlwind months and 92 victories later— Giants fans came unglued.

The cheers drowned out Tony Bennett. Amid the tumult and at Bochy's urging, the Giants took a victory lap around the park. Players high-fived fans, perfect strangers embraced out of relief and in anticipation, everyone smiled and laughed and jumped with joy, and the signs waved: FEAR THE BEARD! SANCHEZ CLINCHEZ! THE TORTURE ENDS TODAY! The corridors of the ballpark rattled with the sweet sound of homegrown love and unexpected joy; a team and its fans united. The Giants were going to the playoffs.

Highlighting the Giants stellar stretch run, Matt Cain averaged better than seven innings in five September starts, winning three and losing none.

Acquired in a trade with the Cubs, Mike Fontenot played three different infield positions for the Giants, left; Santiago Casilla's career-best 1.95 ERA bolstered the Giants exceptional bullpen, right.

No contribution was too small in the success of the 2010 Giants; clockwise from top left: Darren Ford scored the winning run in an important September victory; Guillermo Mota proved intimidating and effective; Dan Runzler flashed one of the team's most powerful and promising arms; and Sergio Romo stepped up as Bruce Bochy's setup man.

Cody Ross won over Giants fans with his grit, smile, and inspired play.

Juan Uribe helped anchor a Giants infield that finished the season tied for the best fielding percentage in baseball.

Despite his cool demeanor, manager Bruce Bochy maintains the passion and fire that marked his nine-year career as a big league catcher.

Trade deadline acquisition Ramon Ramirez posted a 0.67 ERA as a Giant, left; Andres Torres wielded one of the largest bats in baseball, right.

After clinching the NL West on the last day of the regular season, the Giants celebrated with a victory lap around the park.

Given the speed with which Tim Lincecum blazed his way to two Cy Young Awards, and considering the repeated excellence of Matt Cain, it's understandable that Giants fans have had a complicated relationship with the team's other young, promising hurler, Jonathan Sanchez. It's never been as easy with the quiet Puerto Rican, and patience can be tested with pitches that avoid the strike zone. Sanchez ranked fourth in the National League in walks in 2009, an issue he compounded in 2010, when he led the league in free passes.

The knee-jerk reaction saw frustrated Giants fans clamor for general manager Brian Sabean to trade the lefty for a power hitter. Sabean always demurred, turning a deaf ear to the impatient shouts. He knew that Sanchez, when right, possessed nearly unhittable stuff, and the brain trust remained steadfast in its belief that the tantalizing talent in his arm lingered, waiting to be unleashed.

The first starburst from Sanchez came when he threw his no-hitter on July 10, 2009, the first no-no in team history since John Montefusco's 1976 gem in Atlanta. The trick was getting consistent performance on that promise, and it could not have come at a better time than during the Giants unlikely, thrilling run in 2010. The 27-year-old delivered time and again. On August 19 in Philadelphia, as the Phillies eyed a demoralizing sweep of the Giants, Sanchez

went eight innings and allowed just two hits and one run in a win that surely made an impression on the powerhouse two-time NL champions. Seven shutout innings on September 5 at Dodger Stadium earned Sanchez his first career win over the Dodgers and, more important, won another series. And, of course, the five shutdown innings in Game 162—helped by his triple and run scored—locked up the NL West title and sent the Giants to the postseason.

In the playoffs, Sanchez's seven and a third innings of two-hit, one-run ball and 11 strikeouts kept the Giants in Game 3 of the NLCS in Atlanta, setting the stage for the ninth-inning heroics and a come-from-behind win. Even his lesser postseason efforts contained particles of magic: in Game 6 of the NLCS, Sanchez only lasted two innings, yet he singled and scored a run in the top of the third to start a game-tying rally.

The statistics back up Sabean's faith: Sanchez's 3.07 ERA was the lowest among the Giants four starters who pitched the entire season. His 205 strikeouts were second on the staff behind only Lincecum, and despite leading the Giants in issuing walks Sanchez allowed the fewest hits per nine innings of any pitcher in the National League.

Fellow rotation mates Lincecum, Cain, Barry Zito, and Madison Bumgarner were all first-round draft picks. Sanchez was a 27th-round selection out of

Ohio Dominican University. The road he traveled was undoubtedly longer, but being recognized as one of the toughest pitchers in baseball makes the reward that much sweeter.

5 ATLANTA

Sometimes when a team reaches the playoffs, there is a palpable sense of accomplishment, a feeling that the goal has been attained and the season is a success, no matter the outcome. Other times, a team reaches the postseason and finds itself overcome with a surge of adrenaline, visions of limitless possibility, and no good answer for the question "Why not us?" The 2010 Giants, riding a wave of energy into the National League Division Series, bore the distinct whiff of the latter.

As the 91-win NL Wild Card Atlanta Braves came to town for the best-of-five series with the sounds of the Game 162 party still echoing throughout The City, the Giants and their fans came to a startling realization: the pitching staff, so often talked about in terms of tantalizing potential, had come of age. The record-setting performance and jaw-dropping statistics in September left no question: the best team ERA in the Major Leagues, plus the most strikeouts. Matt Cain delivered a near no-hitter in Colorado. Madison Bumgarner posted a 1.13 ERA for the month. Jonathan Sanchez went 4–1 with a 1.01 ERA in the final month.

Then there was Timmy. Manager Bruce Bochy tabbed Tim Lincecum to start Game 1 of the NLDS against Atlanta's Derek Lowe, providing the ultimate statement of Lincecum's meaning to the franchise. After a season in which he endured the roughest

stretches of his career, the Giants entrusted him with leading the way in October and gave him the ball for San Francisco's first playoff game since 2003. Lowe knew of pitching in the postseason; with the Red Sox in 2004, he became the first pitcher ever to win the final game of the Division Series, the Championship Series, and the World Series, delivering Boston's first title in 86 years. For Lincecum, this would be his first-ever postseason start.

No matter. By the time San Francisco resident Robin Williams welcomed his team onto the field while waving an orange rally towel, Lincecum was more than ready. He promptly surrendered a leadoff double to Omar Infante, giving pause to the 43,936 fans on hand, but Lincecum was unfazed and finished the inning unscathed. In the second, he threw nine pitches—all for swinging strikes. He didn't allow another hit until the seventh. Rocking, twisting, and

The Giants—and Brian Wilson's beard—instilled fear in opponents during the playoffs.

contorting his lithe body time after time, Lincecum carved history. His changeup dove, and the Braves chased. His slider mocked Atlanta's bats. On a brisk 61-degree night, his velocity never dipped, staying in the 90s. When Lincecum struck out Eric Hinske to end the eighth inning with a 1–0 lead—Buster Posey

Game 1 of the NLDS at AT&T Park marked the first postseason game in San Francisco since 2003.

The Giants voted to wear their Orange Friday jerseys for Game 2. Pat Burrell got things going with a first-inning three-run homer off Tommy Hanson, and Matt Cain pitched six and two-thirds strong innings, allowing just one unearned run. Carrying a 4–1 lead into the eighth inning, the NLDS could not have been going better. And then it all went so wrong so fast. The Braves rallied for three gut-wrenching runs, and the game went to extra frames. Posey had a chance to produce magic with the bases loaded and one out in the tenth inning, only to ground into a double play. Atlanta pitcher-turned-outfielder Rick Ankiel jacked one out in the eleventh, and the Braves, who led the Majors in comeback wins in 2010, stole the game, 5–4. Given lingering memories of NLDS road exits in 2000 and 2003, Giants fans hoped the loss would not prove a momentum or spirit crusher, though those fears would prove unfounded come Game 3, one of the most significant turns of fate in Giants history.

The details jangle nerves, even in the retelling. Starting pitchers Tim Hudson and Jonathan Sanchez both threw stellar games, and the Giants lefty fanned 11 Braves in seven and a third innings before exiting the game with a runner on first base and 1–0 lead. The next batter, Eric Hinske, promptly blasted a two-run home run to give the Braves a 2–1 lead, delivering a blow that sickened Giants fans and sent Turner Field into apoplexy.

Three outs away from facing an elimination game on the road, Cody Ross popped out. One down. Pinch hitter Travis Ishikawa somehow concentrated enough amid the cacophony to draw a walk off Craig Kimbrel. Andres Torres struck out. Two down. With the stadium rocking and TV cameras shaking and Kimbrel throwing 96 mph and two strikes against Freddy Sanchez, Kimbrel decided to throw a changeup, and Sanchez stayed back, not fooled by the off-speed pitch, and lined a single up the middle.

had scored the lone run after a single, his first-ever Major League stolen base, and a Cody Ross RBI single—the question on everyone's mind was whether or not Bochy would send Lincecum back out or Brian Wilson in to close it.

The fans made their opinion clear with deafening cheers for Lincecum to take the field. In the stands, one lifelong Giants fan felt the rush of a flashback. Former Journey lead singer Steve Perry admitted he got goose bumps, knowing firsthand the feeling of standing in the wings getting set for an encore. When Lincecum emerged from the dugout to pitch

the ninth ("Never a doubt," said Bochy), he was the rock star heading back out onstage to the frenzied delight of an adoring throng. It was a sign that the 2010 playoffs would bear the Giants stamp.

Fittingly, Lincecum ended it with a strikeout on his 119th pitch. The line: nine innings, two hits, one walk, and a franchise-postseason-record 14 strikeouts. Call it tone setting or foreshadowing or simply epic; all were appropriate descriptions. "There was a lot of electricity out there," Posey said. "When you throw a complete-game shutout with 14 Ks, it's going to get pretty loud."

New life. The Giants not only lived, they rose. Huff raked what he called "the biggest hit of my life" off Mike Dunn, scoring Ishikawa to tie the game. Posey hit a ground ball to Brooks Conrad at second base, only Conrad booted it for his third error of the game. Sanchez scored and, against all probability, the Giants went on to win, 3–2. Speaking to the first postseason ninth-inning comeback win in franchise history, the ever-understated Bochy called it "a great win."

Content in the knowledge that the Giants, at worst, would return home for Game 5, Bochy did not have to make the decision to start Lincecum on short rest and instead gave the Game 4 nod to Bumgarner. The youngest starting pitcher in Giants playoffs history went six innings, allowing only two runs. Against the Braves' seasoned veteran Lowe, the Giants twice overcame deficits; first when Ross broke up Lowe's no-hit bid with a home run in the sixth inning, then again in the seventh when Ross singled in Posey for the go-ahead run. Santiago Casilla, Javier Lopez, and Brian Wilson slammed the door for a three-games-to-one series win—all one-run games—and a ticket to the Giants fifth NLCS.

Spraying champagne in the clubhouse for the second time in eight days, Ross's ever-present smile grew doubly wide as he spoke for not only his team-mates but also Giants fans everywhere: "Who'd have thought it?"

Cheers erupted back in the Bay Area as the faith-ful looked forward to a shot at the bully: the Phillies, two-time defending National League champions, would be favored by anyone not clad in orange and black. The movement was gaining steam. On the night of Game 3, the singer Ashkon and the White Collar Brawlers posted on YouTube a video set to the tune of the Journey smash hit "Don't Stop Believin'." It instantly went viral across Facebook and Twitter (2,000,000 views to date), and Giants fans adopted an anthem, singing along: *Don't Stop Believin'/ This could be the season!*

Aubrey Huff made the most of his first postseason, keying a Giants victory in Game 3 with a ninth inning RBI.

One of baseball's most recognizable mascots, Lou Seal joined the Giants in 1996, left; Bill Neukom, looking on before Game 1, took over as managing general partner and CEO in 2008, right.

Third base coach Tim Flannery played in the 1984 World Series with the Padres, along with teammate Bruce Bochy.

Buster Posey's one and only stolen base of the 2010 season came at a critical time in Game 1.

Posey's steal put him in position to score what proved to be the game-winning run when Cody Ross came through with a clutch single.

The intensity of Game 2 kept the Giants out of their seats and on their feet.

For the second straight season Giants pitchers lead the Major Leagues in strikeouts and kept the fans in the arcade busy.

After scoring four runs in the first two innings of Game 2, the Giants bats fell silent and the Braves went on to win in extra innings.

For the proper context of Matt Cain's journey from 20-year-old rookie phenom to 26-year-old World Series champion, consider the landscape on the day he made his Major League debut as a Giant. The starting lineup featured Randy Winn, Omar Vizquel, J. T. Snow, Moises Alou, Ray Durham, Pedro Feliz, Todd Linden, and Mike Matheny. Kirk Rueter, Jason Schmidt, Noah Lowry, and Brett Tomko made up the rotation. Barry Bonds, playing only 14 games that year because of injuries, was gone but not forgotten.

In other words, Cain is from a bygone era in Giants history. A hot prospect selected in the first round of the 2002 draft, the high school fireballer from Germantown, Tennessee, symbolized the organization's renewed commitment to homegrown pitching, a new face, a new direction. Only Cain would have to wait to see that direction take shape. And it was a long wait.

His rookie year, 2005, was the first of four consecutive losing seasons for the Giants, a stretch of futility that tied the worst stretch in San Francisco history (1974–77). All the while, the 6-foot-3-inch pitcher with the sturdy frame, baby face, and commanding mound presence delivered brilliance, time and again. Still, he would wait, patiently, believing in the promise of the eventual reward.

By the time help arrived—most notably when Tim Lincecum joined the team in 2007—Cain had matured into a veteran, a quiet leader who earned such respect for his work ethic and humility that he was voted the 2009 recipient of the Willie Mac Award, the team's highest honor, bestowed by the players to their most inspirational teammate.

In 2010 Cain proved the Giants most consistent starter with a team-high 223-1/3 innings and a team-low 1.084 WHIP (walks plus hits per innings pitched). Come October, his epic performance earned Cain a place among the game's all-time greats, as he became just the fourth pitcher in history to throw 20 or more postseason innings and not allow an earned run. One more statistic to illustrate the consistent brilliance of the guy they call Cainer: he is one of only four pitchers in the past four years to log at least 200 innings per season and post a sub-4.00 earned run average. (Roy Halladay, C. C. Sabathia, and Dan Haren are the others.)

But ask Cain about it, and he'll do as he did after his World Series Game 2 gem: credit his catcher for calling the game, credit his defense for making plays, and credit his offense for scoring the runs.

The fact that the unorthodox, offbeat Lincecum draws more shrieks from fans and adulation from the press has never been lost on Cain, yet one of his most important contributions to the franchise is never having let envy intrude on the clubhouse fabric. At the World Series victory parade at city hall, afforded the

opportunity to speak, Cain chose to thank the parents and coaches and friends who helped all the players along the way. It was a characteristically mature response from the longest-tenured Giant.

By the time Game 1 of the National League Championship Series began in Philadelphia on Saturday, October 16, the Giants had assumed their identity courtesy of manager Bruce Bochy. Never mind the best pitching staff in the Majors; instead, citing the circuitous career paths of players like Aubrey Huff, Pat Burrell, Juan Uribe, and Cody Ross, Bochy laughingly called his crew "castoffs and misfits."

The ragtag image fueled the nation's perception of the Giants chances against the Phillies, owners of 97 wins, home-field advantage, and back-to-back NL crowns. A perfect 10 out of 10 "experts" on ESPN picked the Phillies to win the series.

The picks were conventional given Philadelphia's vast talent. With the off-season acquisition of eventual Cy Young Award winner Roy Halladay, who threw a perfect game in May 2010, then a no-hitter against Cincinnati in the NLDS, plus the midseason addition of veteran pitcher Roy Oswalt, the Phillies' rotation rivaled the Giants. Philadelphia also had something the Giants did not: big bats, and lots of them, notably Ryan Howard, Jayson Werth, and Chase Utley. Yet the NLCS would prove that the Phillies—and baseball fans and pundits everywhere—would underestimate the Giants at their own peril. After all, the Giants had scratched out three victories during the regular season against Halladay, Oswalt, and the Phillies' third ace, 2008 World Series MVP Cole Hamels. "They have

big-name pitchers," said Jonathan Sanchez, "but we also have big-name pitchers."

There is no bigger name for the Giants than Tim Lincecum, and Bochy went with his ace in Game 1. Phillies manager Charlie Manuel countered with Halladay, and the media hyped the game as one of the greatest October pitching duels ever. It played out that way before a crowd of 45,929 until the top of the third inning, when Halladay, after retiring the first seven Giants, tried to sneak an inside fastball past Cody Ross. *Boom!* Ross launched it into the left field seats for a 1–0 Giants lead. It was a startling blow, an awakening blow. Adrenaline surged—doubly so when Ross unfathomably repeated the feat in the fifth inning, this time blasting a homer off Halladay even deeper into the left field seats.

Giants fans watched with a mix of euphoria and blissful perplexity: Cody Ross? Two home runs? Off Roy Halladay? In Philadelphia? In the NLCS? The 5-foot-10-inch, 29-year-old outfielder with a

Deafening cheers greeted Barry Bonds before Game 3, above, **and Aubrey Huff as he scored the winning run in Game 4,** right.

shaved head and a beard, a Giant for less than two months, was fast becoming a legend.

Infused with the strength of Ross's heroics, Lincecum pitched seven innings, allowing three runs. Lefty specialist Javier Lopez retired Utley and Howard consecutively and impressively in the eighth inning, and RBIs from Burrell and Uribe added to the final 4–3 tally that gave the underdog Giants a one-game lead in the best-of-seven series.

The official attendance at Game 4 was 43,515, not including kayakers in McCovey Cove.

The next morning, the *San Francisco Chronicle* headline trumpeted Ross's achievements: TWO JACKS TRUMP ACE. Ross homered again in Game 2, but it was the team's only run, and the Giants would fly home, settling for a split after Oswalt dominated San Francisco with eight innings of three-hit ball in a 6–1 Phillies win.

Game 3 was fortuitously scheduled as an afternoon start, allowing 43,320 Giants fans to enjoy AT&T Park in the balmy autumn sunshine and watch meaningful October shadows creep across the diamond. The fans were psyched; a boat in McCovey Cove even flew a giant red "Rally Thong" atop its mast. Matt

Cain outpitched Hamels in a 3–0 Giants win, turning in seven innings of scoreless ball. It was Ross, naturally, who drove in the game's first run with a double down the left field line, sliding into second amid chants of *Co-dy! Co-dy!* from a crowd that increasingly grasped the momentousness of the proceedings. Cain exited to thunderous applause, never changing his expression, the stoic warrior.

Up two games to one in the series, the Giants entered Game 4 expecting a battle—not the most epic ballgame in the history of China Basin. So intertwined were the developments that selecting a particular moment or highlight undermines the

intricacy, but this much is true: Buster Posey played the game of his life, roping four hits and delivering clutch defense in the fifth inning when he cleanly picked a one-hop throw from outfielder Aaron Rowand and made a sweeping tag to nail Carlos Ruiz and prevent a Phillies run. Bochy started a slumping Pablo Sandoval for the first time in six games, and he answered the call with an electrifying two-run double in the sixth inning to give the Giants a 5–4 lead. Safe on second, Panda lifted his arms skyward then pointed at a dugout exploding with joy.

The Phillies would tie the game in the eighth inning, then Bochy executed a double-switch in the top of the ninth, bringing Juan Uribe in to play shortstop and hit fourth and Brian Wilson in to pitch. The Phillies went down in order in the top half of the frame then sent Oswalt out to pitch the bottom of the ninth. With one away, Huff on third base, and Uribe at the plate, the clutch veteran lofted a fly ball to left field; Huff tagged, churning toward home plate, teeth clenched, arms pumping, sliding in with a fist pump held high.

Ball game. The Giants dugout emptied, and AT&T Park shook to its moorings. The players mobbed Uribe, a beloved player whose cousin, the late Jose Uribe, was a fixture at shortstop and a fan favorite during the 1980s "Humm Baby" era. Juan Uribe, who rarely gives interviews in English, has a phrase for such moments: "A lot of happy." Indeed.

The proud Phillies denied the Giants a chance to earn a World Series berth in San Francisco, taking Game 5 and the Halladay vs. Lincecum rematch by the score of 4–2, sending the series back to Philadelphia. Clinching a League Championship Series on the road, especially in the den of the champion, is a daunting task. Philly fans came out in force for Game 6 ready to will their heroes back to the World Series for the third year in a row. Trying everything to rile the visitors, they picked on Giants starter Jonathan Sanchez from the get-go, singing *Sannnnn-chezzz.* Whether it was the fans or the Phillies

Members of the inaugural 1958 San Francisco Giants threw out the ceremonial first pitch before Game 5: Willie Mays, Orlando Cepeda, Jim Davenport, Felipe Alou, and Eddie Bressoud.

or both, by the top of the third inning, San Francisco trailed 2–0. Unimpressed, the Giants responded by scraping together two runs on a rally started by Sanchez, who bested opposing starter Oswalt with a base hit and a run scored on RBI by Huff.

The importance of the game and its attendant emotions began to take hold. Innings crackled with tension. Who would falter first? Jeremy Affeldt entered the game in the bottom of the third inning and threw two critical scoreless innings. In a daring move, Bochy summoned starter Madison Bumgarner to pitch the fifth and sixth innings in relief. The 21-year-old put up nothing but zeroes.

In the eighth inning, Phillies reliever Ryan Madson threw a two-out first-pitch slider to Uribe that caught too much of the plate. Uribe popped it high to right field, and as Werth went back and looked up, what at first appeared to be a lazy fly ball proved both true and sudden: a home run to give the Giants a 3–2 lead.

The gasp, then silence, of 46,062 Phillies fans hung in the air. Uribe received a hero's welcome—high 10s, bear hugs, and war whoops in the dugout, all caught on TV microphones. Once again, Brian Wilson needed to be at his best when stakes were highest. Ever adventurous, Wilson walked two, putting the tying run in scoring position and bringing slugger Ryan Howard

to the plate. In a scene played out in countless backyards—bottom of the ninth, two outs, full count—Wilson zinged a backdoor slider. Home plate umpire Tom Hallion called strike three, ringing up Howard with a flourish.

For only the fourth time since moving to San Francisco in 1958, the Giants were going to the World Series. Managing partner Bill Neukom accepted the Warren C. Giles Trophy presented to the champions of the National League, hoisted it aloft, and, as if answering the doubters who actually believed the Giants were nothing more than castoffs and misfits, proclaimed with joy, "How about *that*?"

The umpiring crew gets set for Game 3.

Buster Posey in a quiet moment before his unforgettable performance in Game 4.

A go-ahead RBI double off Cole Hamels in Game 3 helped Cody Ross earn MVP honors for the NLCS.

In the eighth inning of Game 3, reliever Javier Lopez set down Phillies sluggers Chase Utley, Placido Polanco, and Ryan Howard in order.

In the NLCS, Andres Torres had seven hits, including three singles in the decisive Game 6.

Matt Cain's dominating postseason run continued with seven shutout innings in Game 3.

Posey made the play of Game 4, snaring a one-hop throw from outfielder Aaron Rowand and making a sweeping tag to nail Carlos Ruiz at the plate.

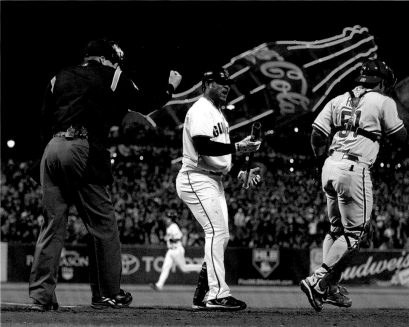

Scenes from the NLCS; clockwise from top left: tickets were a hot commodity when the playoffs returned to AT&T Park; Jeremy Affeldt pitched two critical shutout innings in Game 6; Juan Uribe fell victim to 2010 Cy Young Award winner Roy Halladay; Madison Bumgarner started Game 4 then came on relief in Game 6.

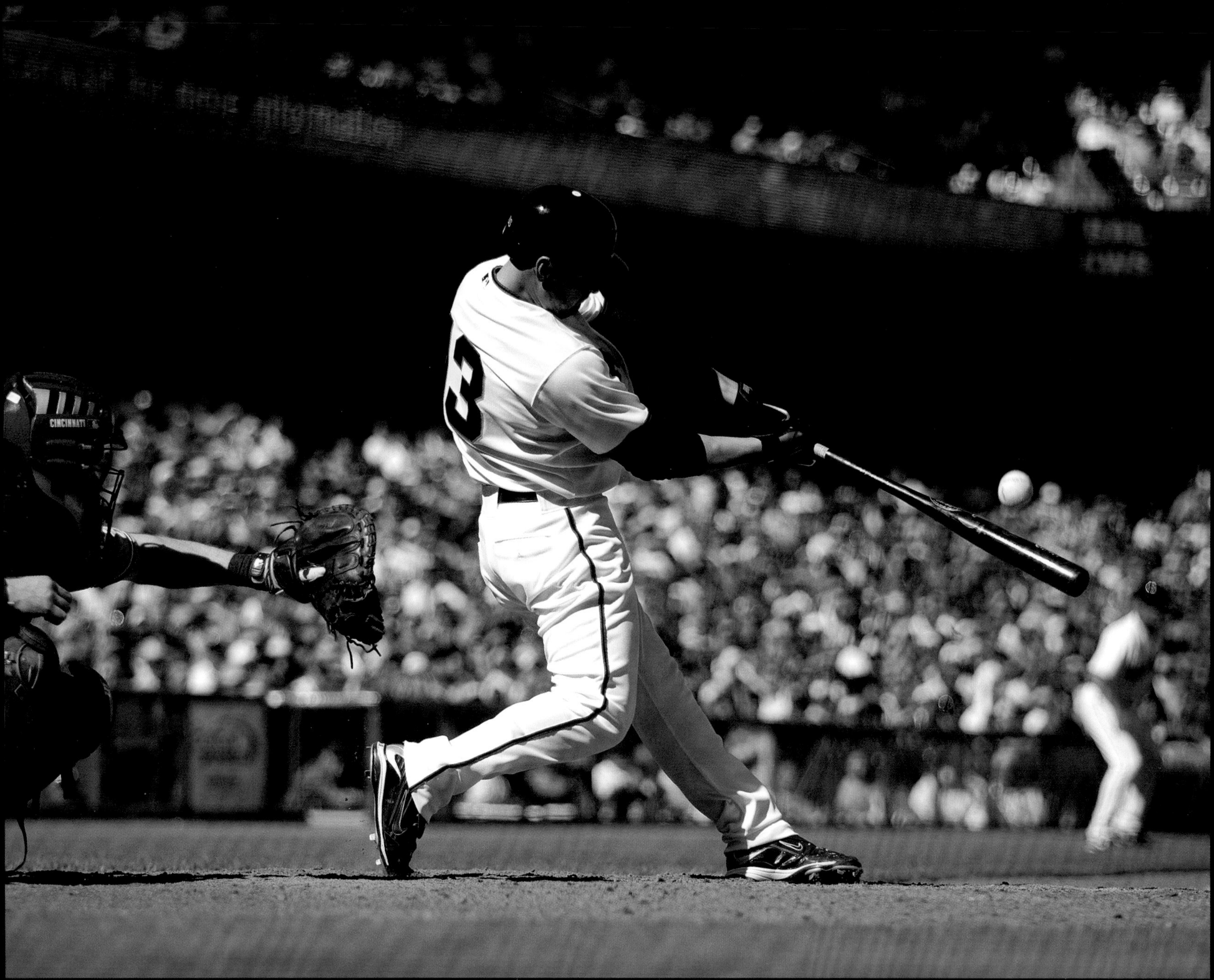
CINCINNATI

Had a Giants fan taken a two-month trip to a desert island during August and September, imagine the surprise upon returning in October to find that the Giants were not only in the NLCS against the Phillies, but also hosting Game 3 at AT&T Park, where the starting right fielder was a less than statuesque Florida transplant who had inspired an iconic painting of his bald head in San Francisco, as well as myriad signs made by adoring fans with slogans like ROSS IS BOSS and ROSSTOBER. That fan would be rightfully struck by a kind of weird parallel universe.

Such is the wonderment of the Cody Ross phenomenon. Dubbed the "Accidental Giant" when the Marlins, to the surprise of many, let Ross go after Giants GM Brian Sabean placed a preemptive waiver claim to block Ross from the rival Padres, Ross wound up the sort of unlikely folk hero that makes sport the beautiful unscripted theatre it is.

For his part, Sabean said that even with an already crowded outfield he would not have put in the claim for Ross if he didn't believe there was a chance Florida would grant the claim. And why not? Ross can play. The 29-year-old New Mexico native may be undersized at 5 feet 10 inches and 195 pounds, but he belted 22 home runs in 2008 and 24 more in 2009. Still, the Giants trade for Jose Guillen's veteran bat nine days before acquiring Ross seemed to have precluded any need for yet another outfielder. But in what may go down as the most important decision made by the

team's brass, the Giants left Guillen off the 25-man playoff roster and handed right field to Ross.

Cue the fireworks: in Game 4 of the NLDS at Atlanta, Ross homered in the sixth inning to break up Derek Lowe's bid for a no-hitter, and then in the seventh he drove in what proved to be the game-winning run in the series clincher. His work in the NLCS was instant lore: two monumental home runs off Roy Halladay in Game 1; a homer off Roy Oswalt in Game 2; the RBI single to break up a scoreless game in the Giants Game 3 victory. Ross hit .350 with three home runs and six extra-base hits in the NLCS to earn series MVP honors.

"I wish you hadn't been claimed by the Giants," half joked Bill Giles, the honorary National League president—and chairman of the Phillies—as he presented Ross the crystal trophy. In accepting the honor, Ross, who grew up dreaming of becoming a rodeo clown, said, "Two months ago, I thought I'd be sitting on the couch watching another team celebrate. I can't thank the Giants enough."

It was fitting that Ross was on base, after yet another clutch postseason hit, on that November night in Texas when Edgar Renteria launched the home run that won the World Series. Scoring ahead of Renteria, Ross, nicknamed "Smiles" by his Giants teammates for his exuberance and perma-grin, jumped high and landed on home plate with gusto, an exclamation point to the two short months during which he became one of the more popular Giants in recent history.

The love was mutual. "Playing in front of that crowd every day," Ross said, "I can't see any place I'd rather be." True to his words, the arbitration-eligible Ross opted to re-up with the Giants. As usual, Aubrey Huff found the comedy in it all. "Great garbage find," he said of Ross, whose contributions would prove invaluable.

While Giants fans exulted in the slaying of the Philadelphia dragon and the new National League champions soaked one another in celebratory champagne, a graphic emblazoned on national television: *Longest World Series Droughts*. The Giants ranked third, their last title dating to 1954 when players named Monte Irvin, Dusty Rhodes, and Willie Mays wore the orange and black and played in the Polo Grounds as the New York Giants. Only the Cleveland Indians (1948) and the Chicago Cubs (1908) eclipsed the Giants futility. Giants fans needn't be reminded.

Giants fans dressed to the nines for just the fourth World Series in San Francisco history.

That it might be the 2010 team who ended the torture was a delightfully odd thought. Could the "castoffs and misfits" achieve what Mays, McCovey, and Cepeda didn't? Will Clark, Matt Williams, and Kevin Mitchell couldn't win the big one, but a team Bruce Bochy jokingly called the "Dirty Dozen" might? Barry Bonds and Jeff Kent came within eight outs of bringing home the hardware only to come up short, but Brian Sabean's patchwork roster of underappreciated overachievers had fans chanting "*Co-dy!*" and "*U!-Ribe!*" and dotting the ballpark with FEAR THE BEARD signs and waving rally thongs. It all happened so curiously fast and felt so incredibly good.

The road to glory would have to go through Texas. The American League champion Rangers represented a worthy foe, no doubt. Manager Ron Washington's AL West champs won 92 games and beat the Tampa Bay Rays and New York Yankees to reach the Fall Classic. Giants pitchers would have their work cut out against a squad that was anchored by eventual league MVP Josh Hamilton and had led all of baseball in hitting. It was a juicy matchup on paper; it just wasn't the one that most people wanted to see. "The whole world wanted the Yankees and the Phillies," Aubrey Huff said, "But it's time for new blood."

The media focused on two key storylines: Texas starter Cliff Lee, one of the all-time great postseason pitchers with a spotless 7–0 record and 1.26 ERA in playoff and World Series games; and Bengie Molina, the Giants beloved former catcher, who was traded to Texas on July 1. Molina called the sensation of facing his old team "a weird, happy feeling." Molina received a rousing welcome from the 43,601 fans jammed into AT&T Park for Game 1, but it was nothing compared to the deafening roar that greeted the Giants lineup: Andres Torres, CF; Freddy Sanchez, 2B; Buster Posey, C; Pat Burrell, LF; Cody Ross, RF; Aubrey Huff, 1B; Juan Uribe, 3B; Edgar Renteria, SS; and Tim Lincecum, P.

The inclusion of Renteria in the starting nine was pure Bochy. Even though the 35-year-old had endured a disappointing, injury-filled season, lowlighted by going 1-for-17 in the NLCS, Bochy believed in veterans—especially one who'd delivered the World Series–winning hit in Game 7 for the Florida Marlins in 1997.

Giants Hall of Famers took the field before Game 1: Willie McCovey, Orlando Cepeda, Monte Irvin, Gaylord Perry, and Juan Marichal.

In Game 1, Lee vs. Lincecum I generated the same intense hype as Halladay vs. Lincecum I and II in the NLCS. But pitching on the game's biggest stage, an amped Lincecum quickly surrendered two runs to put the Giants in an early hole. A recording of Tony Bennett singing "I Left My Heart in San Francisco" caps every Giants home win, only on this night fans were treated to the soothing melody before the second inning—by the legend himself, live and in person. Perhaps the players were listening, too, as the Giants found their groove and tagged Lee for eight hits and six earned runs, chasing the Rangers ace in just four and two-thirds innings, by far his worst October start ever.

Freddy Sanchez exploded for three doubles and three RBI as part of a 14-hit parade that included a loud, pulsating three-run home run in the fifth inning by Juan Uribe off reliever Darren O'Day. The Rangers tried to make a game of it late, scoring three runs in the top of the ninth, but Brian Wilson finished off an 11–7 victory that not only gave the Giants the early advantage in the Series but also dealt a serious blow to the formerly untouchable Cliff Lee.

Matt Cain started Game 2 the next day under the threat of rain. Wearing his black socks high, Cain mixed his pitches, hit his locations, competed tenaciously, and silenced the Rangers sluggers, giving up four hits over seven and two-thirds innings. In three postseason starts, Cain had allowed exactly zero runs. "He was emotionless," marveled Wilson. "Sheer dominance." It was evident that nothing—rain, hail, tornado—could stop him, save for a call to the bullpen.

When Bochy made the call with two outs and a 2–0 lead in the eighth, Cain walked off the mound to what was arguably the longest and loudest ovation in AT&T Park history. Reacting to the thunderous applause of 43,622 fans committed to the moment, broadcaster and former big league pitcher Mike Krukow said that Cain "will remember that for the rest of his life."

When the first few bars of the Journey classic "Lights" came over the loudspeakers before the bottom of the eighth inning, the crowd needed no cue, singing in joyous unison the Bay Area supergroup's love letter to San Francisco. "*When the lights go down in the City/And the sun shines on the Bay . . .*" When iconic Journey front man and devout Giants fan Steve Perry appeared on the stadium's Diamond Vision screen singing the words, the fans sang louder, and as the scoreboard flashed postcard-perfect images of San Francisco, one could not help but sense that something larger was at work. Maybe this was the place, and maybe this was the time.

The game took a strange but fun turn after Cain left, as the Giants tacked on seven runs in the bottom of the eighth inning en route to a 9–0 shellacking of the Rangers that not only erased doubts among the "experts" who overwhelmingly picked the Rangers to win it all, but also raised the very real possibility that, with two wins in Texas, the Giants had played their final home game of 2010.

Game 3 in Arlington, Texas, marked the first World Series home game in the Rangers' nearly 40-year history. The crowd of 52,419 left happy after a 4–2 win led by starter Colby Lewis, who kept Giants bats in check, and rookie Mitch Moreland, who jacked a three-run homer off Jonathan Sanchez. Game 4, on Halloween, was pivotal for the Giants, as no one relished the prospect of the Rangers evening the series at two games apiece with Cliff Lee set to pitch Game 5 at home. Many fans hoped Bochy would bring back Lincecum on short rest, but the manager stuck with Madison Bumgarner. Texas countered with Tommy Hunter and presidents George H. W. Bush (41st) and George W. Bush (43rd) throwing out the ceremonial first pitches.

Bumgarner's statistics—eight innings, three hits, two walks, six strikeouts, zero runs—are made all the more impressive by the superlatives: he and Posey formed the first rookie battery in the World Series since 1947; Bumgarner became the second-youngest pitcher ever to throw six or more shutout innings in the World Series; and his victory earned the Giants the distinction of the first team since the 1966 Baltimore Orioles to throw two shutouts in the Series. Amid all the pressure, Posey said he'd never been more in sync with a pitcher in any game, ever. Bumgarner, sporting the orange-billed cap the team wore on Sundays in 2010, said he kept telling himself to relax and that

eventually it became second nature. What proved most important about the effort was its heft, as a fearless 21-year-old rookie delivered the Giants to the doorstep of a World Series title.

Monday, November 1. On a perfectly pleasant 68-degree evening in Arlington, Texas, the Giants moved about with purpose in pregame warm-ups, mixing solemnity with looseness. They knew the stakes. Bochy was lighthearted in his chat before Game 6 with the media, though he'd later admit he was so excited the night before that he couldn't sleep.

Lee vs. Lincecum II pitted the Giants shaggy-haired free-spirited homegrown prodigy against the Rangers' quiet mercenary, now playing for his fourth team in two seasons. Lincecum drew inspiration and motivation watching Bumgarner in Game 4; privately, he vowed to pitching coach Dave Righetti that he'd be better this night than in Game 1. Executing with purpose and alacrity, Lincecum was sensational. The game careened into the seventh inning, still scoreless, when Cody Ross—batting cleanup in Bochy's ever-changing lineup—singled off Lee for just the fourth hit of the game. Uribe singled then Huff laid down the first bunt of his 11-year career, moving the runners over. Pat Burrell struck out, and with two outs up stepped Renteria. After falling behind in the count two balls and no strikes, Lee challenged Renteria with a cutter.

In the radio booth, Dave Flemming tracked the ball's flight to left-center field. "It is . . . GONE!" he shouted, his cracking voice snapping the final word into two.

Back in San Francisco, thousands of fans watching on big screens at the Civic Center Plaza erupted with joy. In bars all across Northern California, patrons captured the elation on cell phones and video cameras. Giants fans on hand in Texas hugged and exulted. Ross jumped on home plate, Uribe followed, then Renteria. As he was mobbed by teammates in

the dugout, the veteran's expression barely changed. After all, he'd done this before.

Lincecum, his eye firmly on the prize, pitched eight innings, gave up three hits and one run, and posted 10 devastating strikeouts. Brian Wilson, on in the bottom ninth to protect a 3–1 lead, struck out Hamilton looking, got Vladimir Guerrero to ground out weakly to shortstop, and struck out Nelson Cruz to end it. In customary fashion, Wilson turned, crossed his arms, and shouted in celebration, then turned back and embraced an onrushing Posey and the descending swarm.

In the radio booth, Duane Kuiper described the scene: "They come pouring out of the dugout, circling Brian Wilson . . . dancing, hugging . . . and you can't help but think this group is celebrating for the Say Hey Kid, for Will the Thrill, celebrating for No. 25, and celebrating for you Giants fans, wherever you are. Giants fans: this party is just getting started."

Only one team gets to bathe in champagne four times in a season, and for the first time it was the San Francisco Giants turn. As the players reveled, equipment manager Mike Murphy, with the team since their inaugural season in 1958, watched with moist eyes, then phoned his old friend Willie Mays. After some time, the Giants took the party back out onto the field where seemingly every Giants fan who'd made the trip remained. They chanted "*MVP!*" for Renteria, who was named the World Series Most Valuable Player. They chanted "*Rookie of the Year!*" for Posey, who would go on to earn that coveted honor. They chanted "*Thank you, Giants!*" as the shiny, silver Commissioner's Trophy passed from teammate to teammate, held high.

Crowded behind the third base dugout, fans shared the spoils with the victors, flatly refusing to allow the moment to end. One fan held high a sign that read THE TORTURE WAS WORTH IT.

The stadium lights stayed on, bright, white beacons, in the middle of a Texas prairie illuminating a heavenly scene.

Opposing managers Bruce Bochy and Ron Washington met at home plate before Game 1.

Cody Ross slid home following a Juan Uribe RBI single in Game 2, as the Giants took a 2–0 lead in the series.

Freddy Sanchez made many brilliant plays in 2010, though none more spectacular than this memorable grab in Game 4 of the World Series.

In Game 4, on Halloween night, Madison Bumgarner pitched eight shutout innings and etched his name into World Series lore.

With two outs and two men on base in the seventh inning of a taut and scoreless Game 5, Edgar Renteria stepped to the plate.

Thousands of Giants fans gathered to watch the game on big screens set up in San Francisco's Civic Center Plaza, hoping and waiting . . .

. . . for the moment that the San Francisco Giants ended 52 years of World Series longing.

San Francisco Giants/Andy Kuno

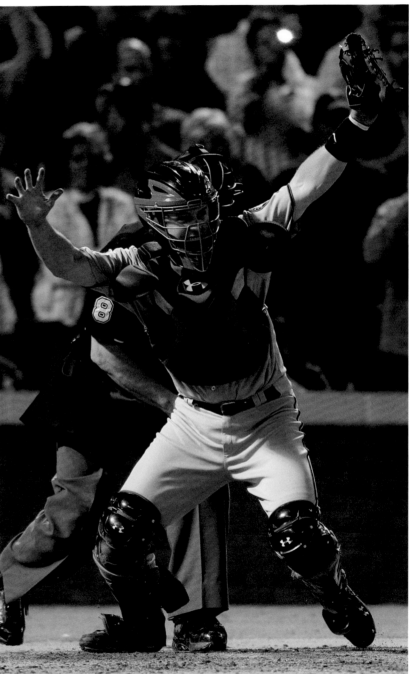

Brian Wilson, fittingly, delivered the final blow, left; Buster Posey clutched the historic last strike then raced to join his fellow champions, right.

The moment when the dream became reality.

The unadulterated joy of a team that believed in themselves when none of the "experts" did.

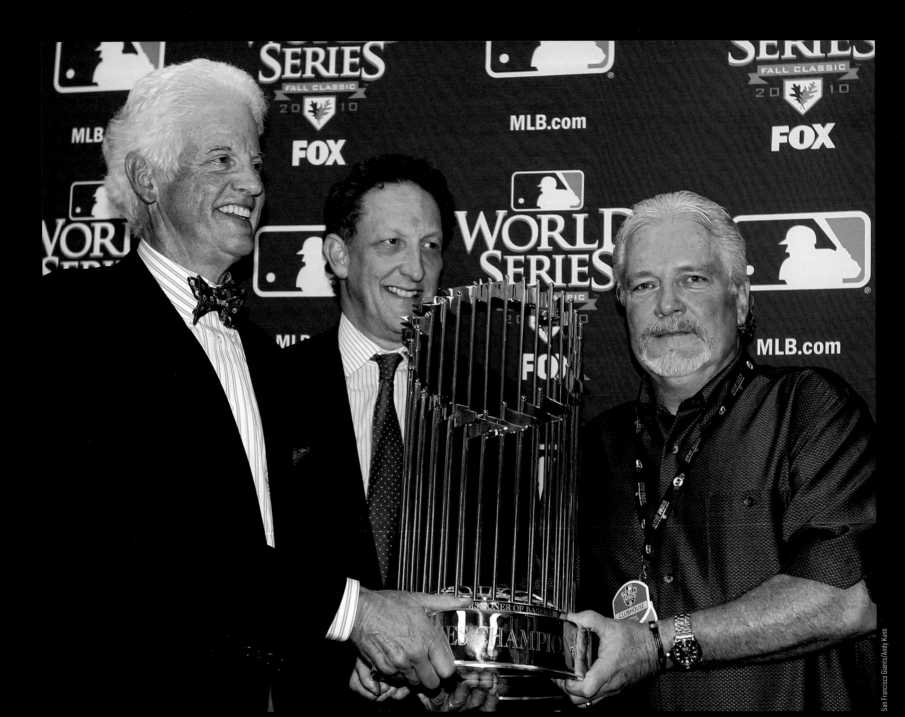

Bill Neukom, Larry Baer, and Brian Sabean all had a hand in delivering the Commissioner's Trophy to San Francisco.

Brian Wilson, left, and Guillermo Mota, right, savor the moment with the ultimate prize.

What *doesn't* make Tim Lincecum so special and different? There's the mop of hair jutting from the back of his sweat-encrusted cap, the pet bulldog named Cy that trots around the clubhouse, the whirl of energy in his windup as he morphs his 5-foot-11-inch, 170-pound body into a captivating blur. That, plus his numbers—sheer devastation—and his awards make Timothy LeRoy Lincecum, or Timmy, Timmy the Kid, the Freak, the Franchise, Seabiscuit—chose your moniker—the man who moves the needle.

In 2010 the San Francisco Giants played a grand total of 177 games. Lincecum pitched the first on Opening Day and the last to win the World Series, making him, literally and figuratively, the alpha and the omega of Giants baseball.

His arrival in the big leagues signaled a paradigm shift for the franchise and new hope for Giants fans. A team that traditionally built on sluggers had drafted two star arms in the first round: Matt Cain in 2002 and Lincecum, from the University of Washington, in 2006. The refocus on pitching reshaped the team's identity, one built for a new era and a spacious ballpark.

Winning back-to-back Cy Young Awards in 2008 and 2009 made Lincecum a mega star in The City, but 2010 would test his mettle. Lincecum struggled—mightily at times, particularly during August when he had no wins against five losses. The fan base felt the angst of his poor performances distinctly and deeply. It was like watching a member of the family flounder and being powerless to help. Critics howled with theories: He's

too small. His body is giving out. His velocity is gone. His hair is too long. No theory was too preposterous. Judged objectively, Lincecum's season totals were excellent. His 16 wins led the team; his 212-1/3 innings trailed only Cain among Giants pitchers; and for the third consecutive year, he led the National League in strikeouts.

Then there was the pride in performance, the flash of dazzling talent Lincecum carried into September—and beyond. Improved conditioning helped his velocity return. He incorporated a slider, catching hitters unaware. His diving changeup remained one of the most devastating pitches in baseball. In addition to posting a 5–1 win-loss record and a 1.94 ERA in September, Lincecum cemented his status in baseball and stature in San Francisco with a virtuoso performance in the postseason, highlighted by striking out 14 Atlanta batters in Game 1 of the NLDS, besting 2010 Cy Young winner Roy Halladay of the Phillies on the road in Game 1 of the NLCS, and twice beating the thought-to-be-unbeatable Cliff Lee in the World Series.

On the final night of the 2010 season, Lincecum handcuffed the vaunted Rangers hitters, allowing just one run and three hits in eight innings. His 10 strikeouts that night made him only the fifth pitcher in history to sit down 10 or more batters in a World Series clincher.

When Brian Wilson struck out Nelson Cruz to give San Francisco its first title (and Lincecum his fourth postseason victory), Lincecum vaulted over the dugout rail like a steeplechase runner. For a moment it

appeared that the suddenness of the move and steep landing angle might send him tumbling. Not Timmy the Kid. Lincecum made an athletic, stylish landing and raced off to join his teammates in celebration.

That gymnast-worthy move, coupled with postgame celebrations punctuated with the colorful and exuberant language of a 26-year-old enjoying the ride of his life, not only made Lincecum stand out that much more, it also made the Giants Superman seem human, just like the rest of us.

AFTERGLOW

The Giants have taken innumerable long-haul flights in the black of night back to San Francisco, but never before with the Commissioner's Trophy riding shotgun. As the team plane jetted back west from Texas, it might as well have been fueled by adrenaline. The trophy passed from hand to hand and aisle to aisle, flashes popping. And when the team bus finally pulled up to AT&T Park, a throng of Giants fans, never minding that it was 3:30 in the morning, roared at the sight of Bill Neukom stepping off the bus with the hardware held high.

The precious metal had a busy off-season, as the World Champions Trophy Tour traveled from San Francisco's gleaming city hall; north to Medford, Oregon; south to San Luis Obispo; east to Reno, Nevada; and down to Scottsdale, Arizona for Spring Training with dozens of stops in between. Paying homage to the franchise's birthplace, the Giants took the trophy back to New York along with the great Willie Mays, who spoke to students at a public school that now stands near the site of the old Polo Grounds.

Fans came out in droves to see the 30-pound hunk of sterling silver made by Tiffany & Co., but the trophy made no more emotional journey than on November 3, 2010, when it rolled through the streets of San Francisco along the World Series parade route to the celebration at city hall.

Before sunrise, with Coit Tower still bathed in gentle orange floodlights, fans arrived, united by their belief—and their joyful disbelief. Streaming into The City, they grabbed spots on Montgomery Street and Market Street and at Civic Center Plaza; the size of the crowd was impossible to count (most estimates were upward of a million) but the mayor's office confirmed it was among the largest public gatherings in the history of San Francisco.

The homemade signs spoke to the varied emotions: DELICIOUS, read one. TIMMY, WILL YOU MARRY ME? read another. THE TORTURE IS OVER.

Workers jockeyed for position in windows of skyscrapers. Fans crowded rooftops and fire escapes. Some climbed trees, others climbed atop city buses. Inconceivable waves of energy and sound engulfed the parade route. Giants players, traveling in motorized cable cars, were visibly moved by the outpouring: block after block, ear-splitting cheers and a sea of smiles. Brian Wilson, in shiny high-tops, mohawk spiked high, and adrenaline coursing, leaped off his cable car and sprinted down Market Street high-fiving fans.

Speaking at city hall, Mike Krukow asked every person in the crowd to think of the person who first told them the story of the Giants.

Aubrey Huff and the magical "Rally Thong."

San Francisco Giants/Missy Mikulecky

He said to thank that person and to keep telling the story, to pass it forward. The resounding cheers spoke to not just the present, but also the future, while one fan's sign summed up all that had passed: DAD, THEY FINALLY DID IT.

The jubilant plane ride home; clockwise from top left: Dan Runzler and Buster Posey; Jonathan Sanchez and Mark DeRosa; Emmanuel Burriss;
Brian Sabean to the right of equipment manager Mike Murphy, who has been with the Giants since the team first moved to San Francisco in 1958.

San Francisco Giants/Missy Mikulecky

A contingent of die-hard fans greeted the Giants in the wee hours of the morning when the team returned to AT&T Park after winning the World Series.

The headline in the Sporting Green—awash in celebratory orange—said it all.

Jeremy Affeldt soaked up the sunshine and warm wishes during the ticker tape parade.

124

The outpouring proved overwhelming for many of the Giants, including Sergio Romo.

Giants fans look forward to seeing Tim Linceum and Buster Posey in orange and black—and World Series victory celebrations—for years to come.

Pomp, circumstance, and the key to The City, presented to Bill Neukom by Mayor Gavin Newsom.

Photo by Brian Haux - Skyhawk Photography

ACKNOWLEDGEMENTS

SKYBOX PRESS

EDITOR
Scott Gummer

PUBLISHER
Peter Gotfredson

CREATIVE DIRECTOR
Nate Beale

COPYEDITOR
Mikayla Butchart

PROOFREADER
Patricia Walsh

SAN FRANCISCO GIANTS

PROJECT DIRECTOR
Mario Alioto

PROJECT MANAGER
Nancy Donati

DIRECTOR OF PHOTOGRAPHY
Missy Mikulecky

RESEARCH EDITOR
Matt Chisholm

BRAD MANGIN I would like to dedicate this book to my Dad for teaching me to love the Giants and my Mom for teaching me how to see. Thanks to the Giants and Skybox Press for having the faith in us to do this book. I am indebted to our brilliant literary agent Amy Rennert who fought so hard to get this book published so our dream could become a reality. My gratitude is also due to Don Hintze, Rich Pilling, and Jessica Foster at Major League Baseball Photos. I was blessed to have many wonderful teachers: Paul Ficken, Terry Smith, Gerry Mooney, Joe Swan, and Jim McNay. Neil Leifer and Carmin Romanelli jump-started my career over 20 years ago. Thanks also to the photo department at Sports Illustrated led by Steve Fine. Picture editors Maureen Cavanagh, Matt Ginella, and Nate Gordon are the best. V.J. Lovero, you were the best there ever was. A tip of the hat to my special supporters: Joe Gosen, Grover Sanschagrin, and my sister Paula Mangin. Brian Murphy did an amazing job putting words to my pictures. John Montefusco, Jack Clark, Mike Ivie, and John Tamargo: because of you I bleed orange and black.

BRIAN MURPHY This book would not have happened without two people. Brad Mangin's idea, energy, friendship, Giants passion and world-class photos made it real, and made it sing. Amy Rennert's tenacity made it happen. Thanks to both. The Giants were gracious, and Skybox Press worked tirelessly. The beat writers—Andy Baggarly, Chris Haft and Henry Schulman—wrote tales that spurred the memory. As always, my wife, Candace, provided guidance and love. You rule, honey. And li'l Declan Murphy provided the twinkle in the eye that makes every day worthwhile. My Mom and Dad are constant inspiration and loved me enough to once get my name on the Candlestick Park scoreboard for a childhood birthday. Thanks, M and D! For the Candlestick generation—for every fan who braved a Friday night in the bleachers, for every diehard who could only land an upper-deck reserved seat for a Dodgers game, for every stranger I high-fived when the Giants scored—this one's for you.

SKYBOX PRESS We wish to thank Bill Neukom, Larry Baer, Staci Slaughter, Tom McDonald, Elizabeth Murphy, Linden Hynes, Dave Martinez, Bonnie Macinnes, Joanne Young and Valerie McGuire at the Giants; Josh Brown, and Jarrett Blass with Major League Baseball; Sandy Hernandez; Linda Clarke; Amy Rennert; Nancy Wolff, Lisa Digernes, and Carolyn Wright; and our sincere thanks to Dean McCausland and Don McCall.

Library of Congress Cataloging-in-Publication Data available.

ISBN: 978-1-60078-656-3

Printed in Canada
10 9 8 7 6 5 4 3 2 1

ENVIRONMENTAL BENEFITS STATEMENT
Skybox Press saved the following resources by printing the pages of this book on chlorine free paper made with 10% post-consumer waste.

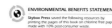

TREES	WATER	SOLID WASTE	GREENHOUSE GASES
26	11,753	714	2,440
FULLY GROWN	GALLONS	POUNDS	POUNDS

Calculations based on research by Environmental Defense and the Paper Task Force.
Manufactured at Friesens Corporation

SKYBOX PRESS 3920 Conde Street   San Diego, CA 92110   www.skyboxpress.com

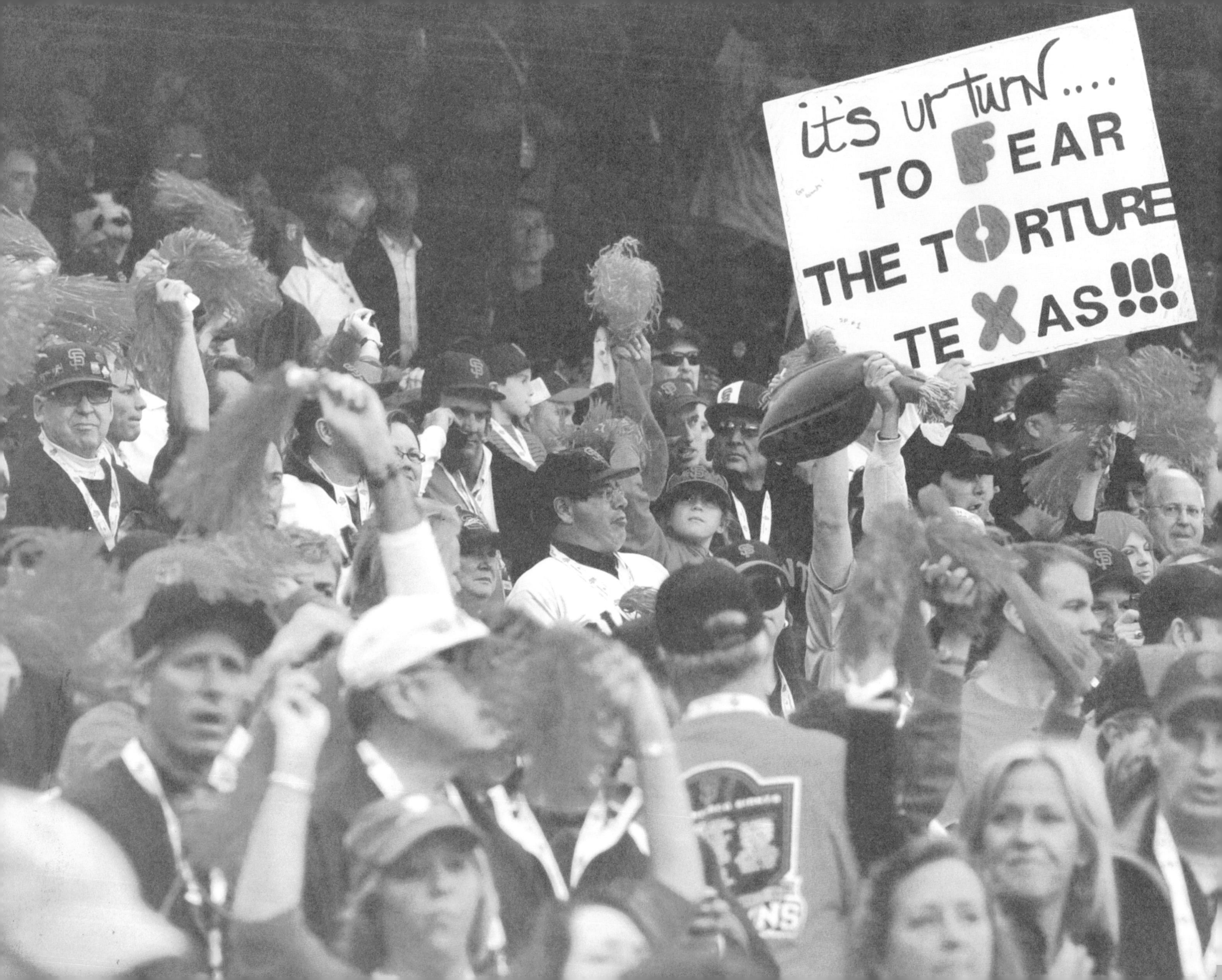
it's ur turn....
TO FEAR
THE TORTURE
TEXAS!!!